> THE MODERN NATIONS IN
>
> HISTORICAL PERSPECTIVE
>
> ROBIN W. WINKS, *General Editor*

The volumes in this series deal with individual nations or groups of closely related nations throughout the world, summarizing the chief historical trends and influences that have contributed to each nation's present-day character, problems, and behavior. Recent data are incorporated with established historical background to achieve a fresh synthesis and original interpretation.

JOHN E. FLINT, the author of this volume, studied at the Universities of Cambridge and London, where he obtained his Ph.D. From 1963-1964 he was seconded by the University of London to serve in Nigeria as Professor and Head of the History Department at the University of Nigeria Nsukka. He is at present Reader in History at King's College, University of London. His publications include *Sir George Goldie and the Making of Nigeria*.

ALSO IN THE AFRICAN SUBSERIES

Central Africa *by Prosser Gifford*
The Congo *by Harry R. Rudin*
Egypt and the Sudan *by Robert Tignor and Robert Collins*
Ethiopia, Eritrea & the Somalilands *by William H. Lewis*
Former French West Africa *by John D. Hargreaves*
Morocco, Algeria, Tunisia *by Richard M. Brace*
Portuguese Africa *by Ronald Chilcote*
Sierra Leone and Liberia *by Christopher Fyfe*

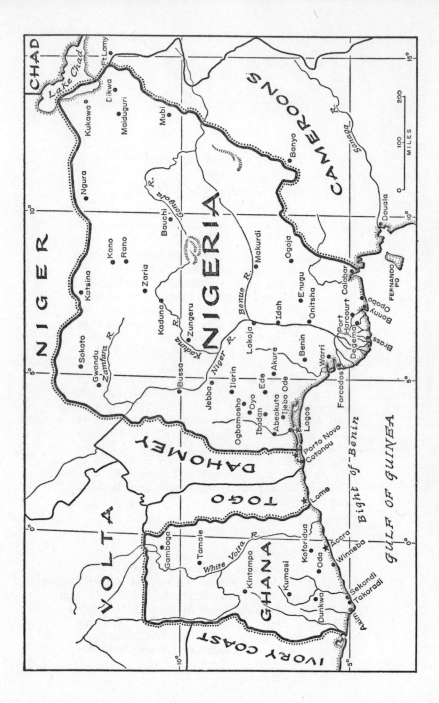

NIGERIA
AND GHANA

JOHN E. FLINT

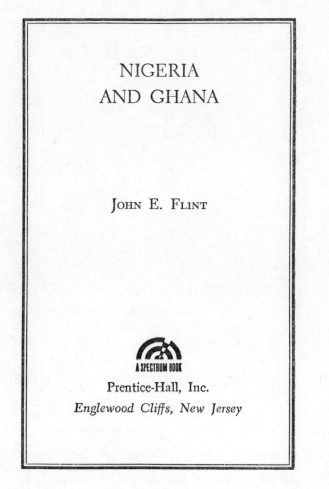

A SPECTRUM BOOK

Prentice-Hall, Inc.

Englewood Cliffs, New Jersey

Current printing (last number):
10 9 8 7 6 5 4 3 2

PREFACE

It is impossible to do justice to the histories of two of the most significant countries in Africa in the space of this short essay, but if this work stimulates its readers to pursue the histories of Nigeria and Ghana in greater detail it will have served its purpose.

The name "Ghana," coined in 1957 to describe the newly independent state which replaced the British Colony of the Gold Coast, is bound to cause a certain amount of confusion in historical narratives, as Ghana was a medieval empire of the western Sudan. I have therefore retained the term "Gold Coast" to refer to the period before 1957.

A work of this kind obviously draws heavily on a multitude of authorities, whom it is impossible to acknowledge individually. To these, and to the very many kind chiefs, politicians, students, and citizens of Nigeria and Ghana who have given my family and me so much kind and patient hospitality, I would like to record my gratitude.

J.E.F.

CONTENTS

vii

NIGERIA
AND GHANA

ONE

The Land, the People, and the Politics

of Independence

Nigeria and Ghana are probably the two most important states of tropical Africa, both because of their present and prospective internal development and because of their roles in the politics and economy of the African continent. Both countries at first glance appear to have passed through similar historic phases: prehistoric colonization by the Negro race; an early agricultural revolution and discovery of iron technology; absorption in turn of Malaysian, American, and European food plants; a similar subjection to the European slave trade; a strong Islamic influence on the northern parts of both countries; a modern period of colonial subjection to the same power, Britain; and nationalist movements which have secured independence. Yet the resulting new nations present many points of contrast: Nigeria is the African giant, her fifty million people being the largest population grouping within a single state in all Africa. Her vast territories are grouped together in a federal, multi-party structure operating through parliamentary forms of government, which in their operation, despite all shortcomings, make Nigeria a land of free speech and free association, and her regime the most liberal in all Africa. At the same time Nigeria's internal and external policies have been marked by a pronounced conservative tendency. In contrast Ghana is a small state (though her population of about six million is respectable by African standards) organized on a unitary one party basis, her parliamentary forms modified to create a presidential system of rule with a strong personality cult. Her internal and external policies appear energetic and radical, with a strain of ruthlessness pervading them. Her more compactly organized population enjoys a higher standard of living than the masses of Nigeria. Despite her smaller population Ghana aspires to the leading role in African international politics, a position which Nigerians often feel should be theirs by right of population and size.

The object of this short study is to trace, through history, the development of these two new states, analyzing the way in which, through apparently similar historical stages, their evolution may be compared and contrasted.

The Geographical Background

It is not possible to understand the history of any part of tropical Africa without considering the more important geographical factors. In Ghana and Nigeria geography has powerfully affected the lives of differing communities, and has done much to create separate areas and cultures within each state. It is not generally realized outside Africa that these countries contain great variations of climate and vegetation, or indeed that the picture of the "hot, steaming, impenetrable jungle" is false. There is no jungle in either Ghana or Nigeria.

Both countries, because they lie in roughly the same latitudes, have an overall similarity of climate. On the coasts the temperature and humidity are generally high, but with a narrow temperature range, usually between 75 and 85 degrees. Further north the temperature range increases, sometimes rising to the 100s in the day and dropping to 60 degrees at night, with lower humidity levels. The seasons of the year are different in kind from those of the nontropical world, being determined not by temperature but by wind changes. Instead of summer and winter, Ghana and Nigeria enjoy rainy and dry seasons. The rainy season extends roughly from April to October, and is caused by moisture-bearing winds from the Atlantic. The rainfall naturally tends to be heaviest on the coast and to thin out as it moves northwards, until hardly any falls on the Sahara fringes. In the dry season, from November to March, the wind veers round and blows from the Sahara, carrying clouds of dry sand and dust known as the *harmattan*. The dust is naturally more severe in the north, and the *harmattan* is shortest on the coast; but everywhere it blows it creates cracked lips, itchy noses, and short tempers!

In the past this climate has been much maligned, especially the wet, steady heat of the immediate coastal areas with which the Europeans first came into contact. The enormous death rate of Europeans before the 1850s gave West Africa the reputation of "the white man's grave," and it was believed that the combination of heat and humidity gave rise to "noxious vapours" which poisoned the blood, lungs, or kidneys. Whereas Europeans generally died, Negroes were supposedly made lazy and idle by the constant heat. In point of fact, however, the climate itself is probably healthier than the severe extremes of Europe or North America, and problems arising from the heat and humidity are technically less severe than those arising from cold in the northern world. The real hazards to health come from the favorable conditions which allow the rapid breeding of parasites which carry diseases, of which the most serious are the mosquito which transmits malaria and the tsetse fly, the bearer of sleeping sickness to humans and of fatal diseases to cattle and horses. In addition there are water-borne parasites, and drinking or bathing in infected water (which for many Africans was until recently the only available supply) can produce various debilitating diseases, usually not fatal, but which created serious physical deficiencies, including blindness.

The tsetse fly has produced some important historical consequences, and has profoundly shaped the economic life of certain parts of Nigeria and Ghana. The tsetse flourished best in the wetter southern forested areas, and not so well in the northern savannah. Since the tsetse is fatal to hooved animals this meant that transport in the forested area could only be by human power until the coming of the automobile and the steam engine. On river systems the canoe provided an effective system for the movement of goods and people, but away from the rivers human porters, carrying goods on their heads, comprised the only system that nature would allow. Such work was hard and dangerous, and naturally fell to the lot of slaves. As a transport system it was limited in scope, so that in the tsetse area, especially away from rivers, African communities and political systems tended to be small in area. In contrast the northern areas, relatively free from the tsetse, could employ the horse, donkey, and camel. State areas could be larger, and political power enforced over distances by the use of cavalry. In turn the need to organize cavalry tended to produce quasi-feudal forms of economic, social, and political organization. Such states were naturally much stronger in the military sense than the smaller units in tsetse areas, but if they tried to dominate them by force they usually found that after initial successes their horses died beneath them and the balance was re-established. The tsetse fly was therefore both a limiting factor impeding the economic organization of the forest peoples, yet at the same time a shield against invasion by northerners, while overall it was a powerful force preventing any single group from forging a large unified state embracing northern savannah, forest, and coastal areas.

The presence or absence of the tsetse, although an important distinction, is not the only determining factor in creating distinct zones and separate cultures. Basic differences in geology and soil structure, modified by the diminishing rainfall moving northwards, produce a complex pattern of differing zones in both Nigeria and Ghana. There are even significant differences in the zone patterns of the two countries, which have affected their histories in no small degree.

Almost the whole coastline of Nigeria is covered by mangrove swamp forest. The mangrove extends furthest inland around the massive delta of the Niger, where it appears from the air like a huge green jigsaw puzzle, cut into pieces by a fantastic pattern of meandering creeks. Further west toward Lagos the mangrove surrounds a great system of lagoons. The mangrove itself is a weird tree which has adapted itself to tidal conditions; its proper trunk is several feet above the water level, and its roots go twisting up above the mud to support it. Almost nothing else will grow in the mud; but where the land rises above tidal level, forming patches of dry land, agricultural settlement takes place. Economically (except for very recent prospects of oil discovery) the region is almost worthless, its only resources being the fish in its creeks. Yet the mangrove swamp has been the scene of great historical activity. It was here that great trading city-states like Brass, Bonny, Opobo, and Calabar were built, for the mangrove belt lay across the river routes to the interior, and by controlling sections of it ambitious Africans could monopolize the trade between Europe and the interior, whether in slaves or, later, in palm oil.

Behind the mangrove swamp lies the Nigerian rain forest, covering most of southern Nigeria to a depth of a hundred or more miles. This is the main productive area of the south, and contains the thickest general concentration of people in the country, who support themselves by root-crop staples like yam and cassava. The forest is divided more or less down the center by the Niger; the western forest is the area of cocoa, rubber, and timber production, whereas the center and the east are the main areas of palm produce which supply the soap and margarine industries of Europe and America with vegetable oil. In earlier times the thick population supplied the slave markets of the New World in profusion. The forest may in earlier times have been thick, even "impenetrable," but it is not so now (except in some government-controlled forest reserves), for human settlement has affected the natural growth, especially on the northern fringes where rainfall is barely adequate to support the forest. This is the result of shifting agriculture, in which plots of land have been cleared by burning off the vegetation, worked until the soil shows signs of exhaustion, and then abandoned for a newly cleared plot. With the high rainfall of the south the forest soon reconquers abandoned plots, but further north—in dryer conditions —grass invades the abandoned plot, tends to catch fire in the dry season, and thereby tree seedlings which might have taken root are destroyed. The main forest once extended much further north than it does now, and its boundary has been affected by human settlement, especially in the west, where the forest terminates about 50 miles north of Lagos. The fact that grassland extends to within 50 miles of the coast at this point has been of great significance in the history of the country, for it enabled southerners in the seventeenth century—because they could use cavalry on the grasslands—to build up in this region the great state of Oyo, an empire rivaling those of the north. It was naturally this area which saw the great struggle between the northern states and Oyo for control of the southwest and access to the sea, and it was here that the northern armies could operate nearest to the coast.

North of the rain forest comes the wide expanse of the savannah country proper extending right up to the northern frontier and the fringes of the Sahara desert. Within this broad area there are grades of savannah. Immediately north of the forest is a zone of what may be described as "derived" savannah, i.e., what was once forest area but is no longer because the rainfall is not sufficient for reforesting after human clearing and burning for agriculture. In the "derived" savannah, grass is dominant, but patches of woodland, and much short tree growth, are very common. Still further north comes the true savannah, more open country with fewer trees, and as the rainfall decreases even more in the far north the country becomes even more open with much shorter grass cover. The agricultural pattern in the north is quite different from that of the forest zone. In the north grains and cereals like sorghum and millet, instead of root crops, are the staples, and cattle play an important part in the economy. In terms of cash exports the north is the great producer of groundnuts ("peanuts") and hides.

Within the north the area of the Jos plateau must be singled out. Much of the northern savannah is over 1000 feet above sea level, and the center of this higher area often rises to more than 2000 feet, but in the Jos area the land rises to an average level of 4000 feet, with peaks of over 5000 feet. Here the nights are cool, often cold enough for warm woolen clothing. This plateau was the location of Nigeria's oldest known civilization (the Nok culture) and seems upon archaeological investigation to be providing the key to the understanding of the ancient history not only of Nigerian peoples and their origins and dispersal routes, but perhaps of many East and Central African peoples of the Bantu linguistic group as well. Many of the archaeological discoveries here have arisen as by-products of one of Nigeria's most modern economic activities, large-scale tin mining, which is concentrated on the plateau.

The zonal pattern of Ghana presents several points of contrast with that of Nigeria. Ghana's coastline has no significant areas of mangrove swamp; indeed the most peculiar feature of Ghana's geography is the way in which, due to a unique combination of wind patterns and rain precipitation on the hills, the northern savannah sweeps around the forest and cuts it off from most of Ghana's eastern seaboard by a narrow strip of savannah actually along the shoreline itself, gradually narrowing from a width of about 50 miles near the Volta River mouth to a few yards near Takoradi. The whole of Ghana's coastline has no natural harbors, and the problem of landing goods and people from ships or canoes in the raging surf was always a severe one until the construction of the modern artificial harbors of Tema and Takoradi.

In general, Ghana, like Nigeria, consists of a northern plateau, which in Ghana is not much more than 1000 feet high, falling in steps to the coast. But in Ghana this pattern is punctuated by the Kwahu scarp, an abrupt ridge running northwest to southeast, with spurs jutting out to the southwest, and terminating behind the coast in the Akwapim hills. This hill system forms in fact a kind of "bone structure" for the forest zone, which terminates just north and south of the hill system, because the hills monopolize rain-precipitation. The spurs to the Kwahu scarp are also the main gold bearing areas. As the forest zone is also the zone of cocoa cultivation, and as gold mining is the main nonagricultural export, the forest zone has assumed an almost complete dominance of Ghana's economic life and, it may be added, of its political life. Geography thus goes a long way in explaining one of the main contrasts between Ghana and Nigeria, for Ghana is a unitary state ruled by southern non-Muslim groups, while Nigeria since independence has been involved in attempting to work out a political system which will give northern Muslims and southern non-Muslims a share in government, and in this attempt it is clear that northern Nigerian Muslims have so far been the dominant political group.

There is one final geographical contrast which should be pointed out. Ghana has several important rivers which flow into the sea on its coastline, of which the meandering Volta is the most important. The Pra, Ankobra, and Tano have also played certain historical roles, but none of these were navigable enough to provide a highway into the interior for European steamships. Nigeria is aptly named; it is the country of the Niger, one of the greatest of African rivers, which despite its complicated delta, proved navigable for steamers in the flood season up to Bussa in the northwest, which its tributary, the Benue, could carry steamers up to Yola in the northeast.

Peoples

Neither Ghana nor Nigeria are nation states in any traditionally accepted sense of the word "nation." The institutions through which their state administrations function are nearly all foreign importations ideologically, their state frontiers are legacies of colonial regimes, and even the English language used in administration and government is not a language used in many homes. Each state is a political unit embracing many cultures and language groups. These cultures differ as much within one state in West Africa—and sometimes more—than do the cultural or language differences between distinct nations in Europe or America. Just as a certain background of geographical knowledge is needed for understanding their histories, so the peoples of Nigeria and Ghana should to be delimited more clearly into cultural and linguistic areas (which often bear relationship to geographical zones). The existence of these linguistic and cultural divisions presents the single greatest internal political challenge which the newly independent states have to face, and the positive task of African nationalism (as opposed to its negative anticolonial role) consists in trying to weld together these often opposed and antagonistic groups into a national unity. These forces of linguistic and cultural disunity, rivalry, and antagonism are usually referred to by Africans as "tribalism," but the concept of "tribe" is not a very precise or useful term to apply to many of the groups involved. The Yoruba, Hausa, or Ibo people of Nigeria each number several million souls, and the Ashanti and Fante of Ghana number hundreds of thousands. All the groups named above could be equally described (as they often were in the precolonial period) as "nations." In fact the problem of unity in both Ghana and Nigeria is really that of trying to create a new "Ghanaian" or "Nigerian" sense of the nation to replace a much older pattern of national groupings based on traditional cultural and language areas.

At first glance it might appear that race would provide some principle of overall unity, for all the peoples of Nigeria and Ghana, with the exception of the important Fulani of northern Nigeria and a few thousand Europeans, Indians, Arabs, and Levantines, are of the Negro race. But the masses of the people feel little sense of "negritude," a sentiment which is confined to a few (and by no means all) intellectuals who have studied or have had contact with the achievements and literature of Negroes in other parts of Africa, or America and the West Indies. Moreover race becomes irrelevant in the face of culture or language, and seems to have little or no impact on either. The Hausa of northern Nigeria are Negro, yet their language is distantly related to the Semitic and Hamitic language families, which are normally associated with "whites." The peoples of Bornu, lying immediately east of the Hausa, though showing a great deal of cultural similarity with the Hausa, speak a language of the Central Saharan family having no relationship whatsoever with Hausa.

There are literally hundreds of language and cultural groups in Nigeria and Ghana, and it would be impossible to categorize them all. However, because certain groups are numerically very large, or sometimes because smaller groups have secured important economic or political power, it is possible to delineate broad patterns showing the main cultural groupings. These groupings in fact play a predominant part in shaping the political scene, especially in Nigeria.

Peoples and Politics—Nigeria

Nigeria is dominated by three main cultural groupings, Hausa-Fulani, Ibo, and Yoruba, which correspond closely to the main geographical zones and to the regional structure of the Federation. These three groups also express themselves in the three main political parties of Nigeria. In the Northern Region the dominant cultural group may be described as Hausa-Fulani, even though the two groups involved have certain racial differences. The Fulani originated in the Senegal area—probably as a result of intermarriage between "white" Berber and Negro groups—and emerged as a "red"-skinned, straight-nosed race speaking a distinct language which is difficult to classify. Essentially a cattle people, they spread throughout the savannah area of West Africa, often welcomed by peoples like the Hausa, who allowed the Fulani's cattle to graze on the land after harvesting for the value of the manure. Later the Fulani began to split into two groups, some Fulani settling in towns, becoming learned and literate in the Islamic culture, intermarrying with the Hausa, and acting as political advisors. These town Fulani, as will be described later, eventually led a movement of Islamic religious revival and revolution which in the early nineteenth century established them as a ruling aristocracy in the north of Nigeria. This position they have maintained through the colonial period and into independence; but by admitting the Hausa to their ruling circles, by intermarrying with them, and by profoundly influencing the Hausa in the direction of a purer form of Islam, they have avoided any serious Hausa-Fulani racial conflict. At present they may be said to represent a single cultural pattern and system of authority in the north, expressed through the Northern Peoples' Congress (NPC), a political party which not only rules the Northern Region, but by virtue of the control of the largest number of seats in the federal parliament, is the dominant partner in the federal government, supplying the prime minister, Alhaji Sir Abubakar Tafawa Balewa, and most members of his cabinet.

The Hausa-Fulani culture and the NPC are very definitely Muslim in inspiration. The same may be said of the large Kanuri people of Bornu. But the southern part of the Northern Region contains many smaller cultural groups which have only been partially influenced by Islam and others which are actively hostile to Islam. In the case of the large group of the Tiv people along the Benue river, this hostility erupted into violence—with attacks on police posts and many deaths—in 1964, along with allegations by the Tiv of political intimidation and attempts at forcible conversion to Islam. In general the Northern Region south of the Benue is not Hausa-Fulani or Muslim in culture, and peoples such as the Idoma and Igala have more historical connection with the south than the north, although their languages are distantly related to Yoruba, the dominant group of the southwest. A slightly different situation obtains further west in the area around the Niger and south of it. Here again the peoples have even more definite historical connection with the Yorubas, and the Borgu and Nupe peoples who speak languages related to Yoruba have played a significant role in Yoruba history. In Ilorin the people actually are Yoruba in every sense. The Borgu, Nupe, and Ilorin peoples, however, have all been profoundly influenced by Islam, and Nupe and Ilorin have rulers descended from Fulani stock. Nevertheless it may be said that the whole area from Bussa to the Tiv country lying south of the Niger and Benue is fertile ground for attempts to break the hold of the Northern Peoples' Congress, and the chief vehicle of opposition is the United Middle Belt Congress (UMBC), which demands the creation of a new Middle Belt Region. If this demand were successful and the UMBC secured control of the new region, this would have profound effects on the national situation, for the UMBC could throw in its lot with the southern parties and displace the NPC from control of the Federal Government.

Even north of the Benue, although the influence of the Muslim religion and the hold of the NPC are much stronger, the culture is not Hausa-Fulani; here the mass of the population roughly south of a horizontal line drawn through the northern capital of Kaduna belongs to a large number of non-Hausa groups. On the Jos plateau there are hundreds of small clusters of peoples who are actively resistant to Islam. The 1952 census gave the following breakdown of population in the Northern Region:

Hausa	5,488,446
Fulani	3,022,581
Kanuri	1,298,306
Yoruba	536,109
Nupe	348,979
Tiv	772,771
Others	5,051,380

In the Eastern Region (which is really the southeastern area of Nigeria), the Ibo group is dominant numerically and politically, expressing itself through the National Council of Nigerian Citizens (NCNC). The Eastern Region is characterized by the almost complete absence of any Muslim influence among any of its peoples, who follow either traditional animistic religions of their linguistic group or Christianity. Literacy and some form of Christianity are almost synonymous here, and the Roman Catholic faith is especially strong among the Ibo. The Ibo people—except on the Niger river, where they came under influence from Benin—never developed monarchical forms of government or "chiefs"; instead they ruled themselves in precolonial times through elders, who interpreted customary law, which was in turn executed by groups of the male population, divided into "age-grades," each age-grade being entrusted with distinct functions such as making war, erecting public works, performing police duties, and so forth. In addition the Ibo society functioned through associations which bestowed titles upon wealthy or able men of achievement, who thereby became respected councillors, though not rulers. The Ibo also assigned an unusual status to their women, who were allowed individual rights in personal property, including trade profits. The impact of colonial rule on this society was remarkable, and of all the Nigerian groups the Ibo have perhaps reacted most swiftly to the challenges of European culture, commerce, and education, though they were the last group in Nigeria upon whom these pressures were imposed. The ancient society gave vent to individualism, and this individualism was even more sharply stimulated by the impact of colonialism. They became the first group to be strongly nationalistic, and large numbers of literate and semiliterate Ibo emigrated to the Northern and Western Regions to exploit opportunities for work in semiskilled trades, truck- and taxi-driving, railway work, clerking, and in the professions (especially law, medicine, and journalism). They have provided a number of outstanding men to the national scene, including the President of Nigeria, Dr. Nnamdi Azikiwe.

The NCNC control of the Eastern Region is complete and now practically unchallenged; because there are no Muslim groups in the Eastern Region it is virtually impossible for the NPC to intervene, and although at one time the influence of Western-Region politics exerted itself by forming areas of opposition, this is now almost dead. Nevertheless the Eastern Regional Government does face problems of unity, though they are less acute than those of the north. More than half the region is occupied by non-Ibo. In the eastern half of the Region there lives a kaleidoscope of small cultural groups, all of whom speak languages related to Bantu. The two main cultural minorities are the Efik-Ibibio on the eastern coastline and in its hinterland, and the Ijo of the Niger delta. Both these groups have proud traditions of dominance over the Ibo—whom they once enslaved and sold to Europeans—and both suffer a sense of frustration now that power has passed to the hinterland. The Efik and Ibibio speak mutually intelligible languages, but their traditional cultures differ in that the Efik, centered on the city of Calabar, were ruled by quasi-monarchical institutions, whereas the Ibibio were organized in much smaller units and ruled by elders. The Ijo are distinct from both, and their language is quite distinct from that of any other people in Nigeria. All three groups, however, have at times expressed their opposition to what they regard as Ibo dominance of the NCNC by voting for opposition representatives at regional and federal elections. In addition there has been support among them for forming a new region to be known as Calabar-Ogoja-Rivers (the COR state), a movement which presents the Eastern Regional Government with a similar situation to that faced by the Northern Government in the demand for a Middle Belt Region. The Ibo, however, are much more dominant numerically in the Eastern Region than the Hausa-Fulani in the Northern; the 1952 census listed 4,918,-736 Ibo in the Eastern Region, as compared with 809,387 Ibibio-Efik, 258,962 Ijo, and 1,038,117 others, mainly the peoples of the Cross River basin area.

When Nigeria achieved independence in 1960 the situation in the Western Region was very similar. Here the dominant group was the Yoruba, numbering some four and a half million people. Their history, as we shall see, had been one of long struggles with the northern Muslims, and of alliances, cultural links, and trade with the peoples of the "middle belt." Rivalry with the north had scarred them deeply and altered their settlement patterns; moreover, they had lost Ilorin to Fulani domination. Islam had also made inroads into the minds of the people, and a large minority were Muslim. It was natural that Yoruba "nationalism," as expressed through the Action Group led by Chief Awolowo, should have an anti-northern flavor, as well as resist the Ibo-dominated NCNC. But the Yoruba have always been the least united of Nigeria's major cultural groups, and opportunities for both the northern and eastern parties were not lacking. The influence of Islam afforded the NPC a base for infiltration, while minority groups within the Western Region gave a like chance to the NCNC. These minorities, located in the eastern half of the Region, consisted of peoples (Edo-speakers, Itsekiri, and Urhobo), who were linguistically and historically related to the Yoruba, but felt themselves nevertheless distinct, together with a large group of Ibo, who were settled on the western side of the Niger. A complex political crisis arose from these pressures in 1962, during which the Action Group split into two parts and Chief Awolowo was arrested, eventually tried, and imprisoned on a charge of plotting to overthrow the federation by force; a new party led by Chief Akintola and backed by the NPC, took over the government of the Western Region, and a 1963 referendum held in the Benin and western Ibo areas endorsed the establishment of a new Mid-Western Region, which fell under NCNC rule in subsequent elections.

The Western Region crisis and the creation of the Mid-West State are of the profoundest significance for the future of Nigeria. By removing all non-Yoruba from the Western Region, the Mid-

West State has rendered the remainder of the Western Region the only unit in the federation with complete cultural and linguistic unity—once more there is a "Yorubaland." The attractions of such a state may cause difficulties in the Yoruba areas which remain in the Northern Region, especially Ilorin. But the future of Yoruba politics is obscure, for the new party of Chief Akintola has never faced the test of regional elections,* and many believe that the Action Group would win such elections under the martyred leadership of the imprisoned Awolowo. Just what will be the relationship between the Yoruba Action Group and the Ibo NCNC is also obscure. The creation of the Mid-West Region has removed the main source of political conflict between the two groups, as was apparent in the Federal Elections of December 1964, when they joined forces to fight the north, only to drift apart afterwards. Moreover, the creation of a new Region is bound to be seen as a precedent for the creation of new Regions in the east or north, especially as the Mid-West Region is so much smaller than the other Regions as to be different in kind. With its small area and its population of only two and a half million, it is essentially a unit of local government, rather than a major unit in the new nation. Dr. Michael Okpara, Premier of the Eastern Region and leader of the NCNC, has already suggested that the future of Nigeria lies in the creation of many such smaller units from the existing Regions, as a means of strengthening central federal control and lessening internal cultural rivalries.

It should now be clear that the main political problem of Nigeria is the fundamental one of how to ensure a harmonious cooperation between widely different cultures, and that this problem challenges the very existence of Nigeria as a state. The three main cultural groups—Hausa-Fulani, Yoruba, and Ibo—are engaged in a complicated balancing act. Almost all the possible combinations necessary to control the federation are pregnant with danger. If the Hausa-Fulani were to use their population dominance and majority of federal seats to exclude southern political groups, the southerners might

---

* Since this book went to press, elections were held in the Western Region (October 1965), whose outcome has been utter confusion, with both sides claiming victory. Chief Akintola retains control, although the Action Group alleges that he is there by fraudulent electoral manipulation.

feel the need to fight for their identity. A Hausa-Fulani-Yoruba combination leaving out the Ibo could lead to an Ibo attempt to secede, for the Mid-West and Eastern Regions, both NCNC-controlled, have the population resources, coastline, and economic strength to become a viable separate nation. The most dangerous of all combinations, however, is the one which in a sense is the most natural: the Yoruba-Ibo "Christian" south against the Hausa-Fulani Muslim north. Such an alliance can only be based on the aim of capturing the "middle-belt" vote and thus destroying the numerical superiority of the NPC. Such a move threatens the NPC in both the federation and the Northern Region and could hardly be tolerated. Failure to capture the "middle belt" would be ascribed by southerners to illegal and undemocratic procedures by the NPC, but short of secession there is little action the south could take. The north would have to try to crush an attempt at southern secession, for northern Nigeria needs access to the sea coast.

Matters have not hitherto reached such perilous extremes, though they have recently come dangerously close to them. Since independence the Federal Government has been a coalition of NPC and NCNC, though it has been clear that the northerners were the dominant partner. These relations, however, are now in a state of tension, and have recently passed through the most acute crisis—beginning with the eruption of the "census issue" and taken almost to the point of destroying Nigeria's unity during the elections of December 1964.

The census question is a central problem of Nigerian politics. When the British withdrew, the federal constitution enshrined the principle that representation in the Federal Parliament should be on a basis of population. Using census figures produced in 1952-53 under British rule (which many thought inaccurate), the north was given 173 seats, the east 74, and the west 62, with 3 more seats for the federal territory of Lagos. Thus the north had a majority of seats, but the NPC chose to eschew domination and admit the NCNC to a share of federal cabinet ministries. Southern politicians expected that a new census would reveal that the northern figures of 1952-53 were too high and that the southern figures would rise to more than 50 per cent of the total, thus allowing a new parliamentary distribution which would build into the situation a *necessity* for the NPC to share its power in the federal cabinet. In 1962 an attempt to take a

new census was made, but the NCNC and Action Group declared that
the figures for the north had been grossly inflated by local census
officials there, and the figures were never officially published. In December 1963 a new census was taken, and this time they were published, by Federal Prime Minister Balewa on February 24th, 1964.
They showed a total Nigerian population of over 55 millions, divided
regionally as follows:

North	29,777,986
East	12,388,646
West	10,278,500
Mid-West	2,533,337
Lagos	675,352

That is, the north still contained 54 per cent of the total population
and was thus to retain its majority in the Federal Parliament.

The publication of these figures, which Dr. Okpara, leader of the
NCNC and Premier of Eastern Nigeria, claimed had been done without consultation of the Regional Premiers, caused an immediate
political storm. While the NPC and Chief Akintola in the west accepted the figures, Dr. Okpara declared that there had been "astro-
nomical inflation" and described the figures as "worse than useless."
Premier Osadebey, the NCNC leader of the Mid-Western Region, regarded them as a "stupendous joke" and the Action Group also condemned them. These comments were met by a strong line from
Alhaji Sir Ahmadu Bello, leader of the NPC and Premier of the
Northern Region, who declared on March 3rd, that whereas he had
no desire to dominate Nigeria, he was ready for a "complete show-
down" if the NCNC and the AG did not accept the figures. A deadlock ensued, with elections for the Federal Parliament due.

There were almost immediate repercussions in the Western Region which were to have a profound effect on the national scene.
Chief Akintola, Premier and leader of the anti-Awolowo Yoruba,
succeeded, with the backing of the NPC, in revolutionizing the situation by detaching most of the Yoruba NCNC members in the Western Region and forming a new party, the Nigerian National Democratic Party (NNDP), to rule the West. The Yoruba NCNC members
who so defected were incensed at what they felt to be Ibo domina-

tion of the NCNC, and there followed a most unpleasant orgy of "tribalism." The Western Government issued a "White Paper" in which it accused the Ibo people as a group of attempting to dominate the country and fill the key positions in Government and the state corporations, such as the railways, with their nominees. The statement was backed by a similar pronouncement, though more moderate in tone, from the NPC in the north. A northern newspaper, the *Nigerian Citizen*, actually carried a cartoon depicting the Ibo as cannibals. Feeling against Ibo residents living in the north ran so high that the Northern Premier had to intervene personally to restrain his people from violence against the Ibo and their property. The intensity of these feelings undoubtedly shocked the more responsible leaders, and by April 1964 there was a tacit agreement among them to drop inflammatory talk and restrain their followers. But the census issue remained unresolved. The Federal Prime Minister held discussions with the Regional Premiers, but no agreement could be reached, and the Eastern Government went so far as to attempt to challenge the census figures in the courts.

The formation of the NNDP in the west now began to show its effects as the Federal Elections drew nearer. The NCNC had stood aside in the original western crisis, perhaps seeing no harm to itself in the destruction of Awolowo and the Action Group. Now the NCNC as a party in the west was destroyed by Akintola, who had openly become an ally of the north and spoke of the "very strong cultural links, social and religious" between the west and north. Such a west-north line-up threatened the easterners with isolation, and even their removal from federal office-holding, so it was natural that they should turn to the original Action Group to redress the balance. The dangerous southern "Christian" alliance against the "Muslim" north was beginning to take shape. By August 1964 it was in being. The Action Group and the NCNC agreed to fight in the coming Federal Elections on a common platform as the United Progressive Grand Alliance (UPGA), to be led by Dr. Okpara, and the NPC formed a similar alliance with Akintola's NNDP, which they called the Nigerian National Alliance (NNA).

The election, scheduled for December 30, 1964, thus became a straight battle between north and south. The object of the southerners was to break the monolithic hold of the NPC on the Northern

Region, especially in the "middle belt." It was soon clear that the election campaign was descending into intimidation and violence. On December 10 President Azikiwe, himself an Ibo and ex-leader of the NCNC, announced that he had received hundreds of letters and telegrams asking him to use his office to prevent victimization and malpractices.

Independent testimony reveals that Azikiwe's anxieties were well-founded. The northerners found it difficult to campaign in the south, and vice versa. The UPGA alleged that 4,000 of its party workers in the north had been arrested, and that 40 of its candidates were jailed so that their constituencies could provide NPC members "returned unopposed" to Parliament. But the worst situation seems to have been in the strife-torn Western Region, where both sides organized bands of thugs, armed with knives and guns, who were driven around the Region in jeeps to terrorize individuals and break up party meetings. As early as August, when the campaign was beginning, the federal riot police tried to stamp out this hooliganism, and in a swift and brilliantly efficient operation thousands of thugs were arrested regardless of their party affiliation and charged with crimes such as assault and illegal arms possession which might have put them behind bars for the duration of the election. This wise move was completely frustrated by Akintola's government, which by administrative pressures succeeded in getting the release of its own "stalwarts," who were now able to operate systematically without fear of retaliation!

As election day neared the Federal Election Commission, the body charged by the constitution with conducting the elections, began to break up. It appeared that a majority of the Commission agreed that irregularities had been serious in many places, but only two of the six members (those from the Eastern and Mid-West Regions) actually wanted the whole election postponed. On the eve of the election these two members resigned. On December 28, two days before the election, the United Progressive Grand Alliance described the election as a "gigantic fraud" and called for a boycott if it were not postponed. The Federal Prime Minister refused to postpone and polling began on December 30, despite the UPGA's boycott. In the Eastern Region and in Lagos the boycott was so effective that practically no polling took place. In the Western and

Mid-West Regions voting was confused and partial, while in the North the election was hardly affected by the boycott. The Nigerian National Alliance of NPC and NNDC thus secured an overwhelming majority, gaining 198 seats of the total house membership of 312.

This was the high point of the crisis, and everything hinged upon the attitude of the NCNC government of Eastern Nigeria, and upon the President of Nigeria, Dr. Azikiwe. Would the Eastern Region attempt to force a reconsideration of the election by threatening to secede? The full story of the crisis of January 1-4, 1965 is not yet known. What we do know is that the President refused at first to call upon the leader of the NPC—former Prime Minister Balewa—to form a government and demanded new elections before he would put cabinet formation in process. For several days there was acute tension and deadlock, until a compromise was reached on January 4 whereby Dr. Azikiwe called upon Balewa to form the federal government, on the understanding that it would be a "broad-based national Government"; when the cabinet was formed three days later four of the seventeen ministers were members of the NCNC. This compromise was essentially a return to pre-election alliances, in which both the NCNC and the NPC abandoned their allies. The Action Group was stranded by the NCNC, and later Akintola's NNDP entered the federal cabinet as reward for its electoral support of the NPC.

As a "solution" this could not have been very welcome to the NCNC, who had failed to shake the NPC hold in the north, and failed even to create a solid UPGA block in the south by securing an Action Group triumph in the Western Region, where Akintola's NNDC had won 39 seats. The NCNC were bound to feel that the result had been engineered by intimidation, violence, and illegal practices. But all they could do to reverse the situation was to threaten secession of the Eastern Region and possible civil war. It seems that Prime Minister Balewa had called the bluff, and that the NCNC, brought to the brink of shattering the federation, had more feeling for Nigerian nationalism than for Ibo "tribalism." The uneasy alliance of north and east in federal politics was therefore restored, but the wounds of the election struck very deep, and one is left with the feeling that this "solution" is more a postponement of the crisis than a resolution of it.

Ideology and Corruption

It should now be apparent that a notable feature of Nigerian political life is the absence of any serious ideological differences between the parties. This arises naturally from the fact that the parties are in essence representative of total regional interests, or at least of the total interests of the dominant cultural group in each Region. This means that they each contain within themselves, in varying degrees, representation of divergent interest groups and ideological beliefs. In general it may be said that the NPC is conservative, whereas the southern parties claim allegiance to socialism. But the NPC's conservatism is a reflection of the conservative social structure of the Region, whereas the "socialism" of the southern parties does not express itself in practical policies of state enterprise or taxation policies designed strongly to redistribute income. Many southern politicians are also substantial "capitalists" in their own right, and have large investments in various Nigerian enterprises in transport, newspapers, real estate speculation in towns, banking, and housing developments; many undoubtedly have investments in European firms operating in Nigeria, besides capital sums invested abroad. Nigerian political issues, therefore, have not polarized around policies to be followed in the social or economic field; all parties believe in "economic development" and encourage foreign "capitalist" investment. Conflicts over economic policies tend to be simply those of geographical rivalry, with certain areas complaining that they are neglected because they are of a minority cultural group.

The absence of sharp ideological differences has undoubtedly helped to create a cynical atmosphere in which corruption has become a major problem. In this respect Nigerian politics may be compared to those of the United States at certain periods in its history, or to Britain in the eighteenth century, when Whigs and Tories struggled for places and privileges. Politics becomes an affair of the "ins" and the "outs," with "floor-crossing" a frequent occurrence, and the more unscrupulous politicians seek the spoils of office for the financial rewards it can bring. With numerous such examples at the apex of Nigerian society, it is small wonder that corruption becomes rife further down the hierarchy. There are already signs of a reaction against corruption, but this too may have its dangers. Hostility and deep bitterness against corrupt politics are very pronounced indeed among the present generation of university students, both those in Nigeria and overseas, most of whom become civil servants and teachers. This feeling is shared by many more mature Nigerians, especially intellectuals who are not directly involved in political life, such as writers and artists, university and grammar-school teachers, and Nigerian technicians. This bitterness often produces a sour attitude towards democratic forms, which are blamed for the prevalence of corruption, and envious eyes are turned to the totalitarian regime in Ghana, which has done much to check corrupt practices. Many yearn for the rule of a strong, ruthless, and incorruptible dictator who would cleanse the Augean stables. Hostility to corruption has also expressed itself through the labor and trade union movement. In 1964 a general strike erupted over the Government's failure to implement the findings of the Morgan Commission on wages, and the strike was characterized by the tendency of local agitators to play on popular resentment of the high salaries, expense allowances, lavish housing, and the expensive automobiles of the ministers and politicians.

On the eve of the publication of this book popular disgust with political corruption and nepotism has found violent expression in the attempted *coup d'état* by Ibo officers of the Nigerian army, which took place in mid-January 1966. The attempt was a result of the chaos and disorder in the Western Region, itself the result of the refusal of AG and NCNC supporters to accept the claim of Chief Akintola and the NNDP to have won the regional election of October 1965. Many of the young Ibo army officers were appalled at the prospect that the army would be called upon to maintain Akintola in power. The widespread rigging, intimidation, and violence which Akintola had practiced discredited the democratic process. At dawn on January 15 the conspirators moved with swift efficiency; the political leaders in the federal and regional capitals were deposed, and many arrested. Chief Akintola and Sir Ahmadu Bello, the NPC leader, were shot. Prime Minister Balewa and Chief Okotie-Eboh, the finance minister, disappeared, and both were found dead a few days later.

Major-General John Ironsi, himself an Ibo, commanded the Nigerian army, and appears to have had no part in the plot. To him the politicians now turned, passing over complete power into his hands to crush the rebellion. But once having done this, the objects of the officers' movement were virtually achieved, and their leader, Major

Nzeogwu agreed to accept Ironsi's authority on conditions that are still being negotiated at the time of writing. General Ironsi has not sought power and disclaims any intention of keeping it, having already set up a commission to revise the Nigerian constitution and restore democracy. The replacement of Nigerian politicians by the rule of the army evoked enthusiastic popular response, especially in the south, and it seems clear that if democracy is restored quickly, it will not be as a result of popular pressures.

Peoples and Politics—Ghana

At first glance it might seem that Ghana would also, like Nigeria, be divided into northern and southern cultural groupings. Northern Ghana bears many similarities to northern Nigeria, for the northern part of the savannah zone is quite distinct from the southern. Its peoples nearly all speak languages of the Voltaic subfamily bearing little relationship to those of northern Nigeria, yet their social and political structures show similarities with those of the rest of the savannah zone, being centralized monarchies with long histories of contact with Islam through the trans-Saharan trade routes. On close examination, however, the parallel with northern Nigeria fails. Islam in northern Ghana never attained the intensity or revolutionary zeal of the Fulani-Hausa culture, nor did it ever seriously threaten the states of the south. The weakness of the northern peoples of Ghana compared with those of Nigeria is, however, basically one of numbers. Whereas the northern peoples of Nigeria comprise more than half the country's population, the northern peoples of Ghana form less than one fifth of the total population.

Moreover, southern Ghana is much more culturally and linguistically homogenous than southern Nigeria. Greenberg has shown that all the peoples of the south speak languages of the same subfamily (the Kwa subfamily of the Niger-Congo stock) as the Ibo or Yoruba of southern Nigeria, but the languages of southern Ghana are even more closely related to each other, nearly all of them being of the Twi branch of Kwa. This does not mean that they are all mutually intelligible—there are three distinct groupings of languages—but the closeness of languages denotes a certain common historical development and very similar cultural patterns. The three groupings are as follows: 1) Along the central part of the eastern frontier there is a complex pattern of many small groups speaking languages of the Twi branch classified as "Central Togo" by linguists. 2) South of this group, and centered on the mouth of the Volta river where the coastal savannah is at its widest point in Ghana are the Ewe group. These were probably late migrants to Ghana from southern Nigeria who, settling at the river mouth, pushed the central Togo groups into the hinterland. Within the group, besides those who speak Ewe proper, are the Adangme and the Ga, the latter being the inhabitants of the immediate area around and including Accra, the capital city of Ghana. The Ga especially, being a group with centuries of contact with Europe and advanced institutions of western education, have been important as an element in the growth of modern nationalism. In recent times they have also tended to throw up splinter groups of a "tribalist" kind which have opposed the government of Nkrumah. The Ewe regard themselves as distinct from the Ga in many ways, and their situation is complicated by the fact that the Ewe group as a whole is split into two by the frontier between Togoland and Ghana, and Ewe in Ghana have been influenced by movements, some of them violent, to rejoin their brothers in Togoland. Similar problems have also affected the group of "Central Togo" speakers immediately to their north. But all of these groups combined cannot compete numerically with the third group—the Akan.

The Akan peoples occupy almost all of the forest zone and some of the savannah north and south of it, about one third the area of Ghana. Numerically they form over 50 per cent of the population, about three million souls. Strictly speaking they are a single linguistic and cultural group, for although they were never politically a unit, their political institutions vary only in detail, and their language is really a single language, broken down into distinct dialects, some of which are mutually intelligible. Since the Akan also straddle the areas devoted to cocoa production and gold mining (Ghana's major exporting activities), the Akan also control a preponderance of the country's wealth.

But although culturally and linguistically one, the Akan were deeply divided by history, and the historical divisions have set the stage for much of Ghana's postindependence politics. These divisions originated with the emergence and rise of Ashanti, a state originating around Kumasi in the late seventeenth century, which expanded north and south in the eighteenth century much as did Oyo in southwestern Nigeria, and then drove down to the sea to gain direct access to European traders in the early nineteenth century. The southern Akan groups, especially the Fante, naturally resisted this threat, absorbing more and more of European culture and techniques in trying to do so. The Fante fell early under British control, and their traditional Akan institutions began to crumble early under the impact. It was thus naturally the Fante who were in the vanguard of the Ghanaian nationalist movement of recent times. The Ashanti, however, though checked by the British in their ambitions to control the coast, developed strong and tough political institutions which delayed their falling under British colonial rule until the very end of the nineteenth century, and even during the colonial period the British themselves did much to preserve traditional Ashanti institutions. Ashanti thus became a stronghold of conservatism, chieftaincy, and traditionalism with a strong distinct sense of local difference. Political rivalry in Ghana thus developed *within* the dominant cultural linguistic group of the Akan. Ashanti conservatism became at times the focus for non-Akan opposition to the ruling group, attracting support from the Ewe and Ga and even from the northern peoples. But this type of opposition, similar in so many ways to what Nigerians would call "tribalism," nevertheless differed in that the basic struggle was within the Akan group. It could thus take on an ideological content which was lacking in Nigerian politics. Ghanaian politics could even take on an aspect of class struggle, in that the traditionalism of Ashanti naturally attracted the conservative elements in society outside Ashanti—men of property, higher education, and aristocratic status in traditional society—whereas the ruling group led by Kwame Nkrumah was based on mass party organization of the "commoners" and stressed a policy of "socialism," which, unlike the "socialism" of the southern Nigerian parties, expressed itself in policies and practices designed to secure state control of the economy, planned economic growth, egalitarian social policies, and the destruction of the influence and privileges of previous elite groups, whether traditional chiefs or the British trained intelligentsia. Moreover the unchallenged dominance of the south, coupled with the cultural and linguistic homogeneity of the Akan, meant that nationalism in Ghana could be much more thorough than in Nigeria, which needs to reconcile powerful regionally-based cultural groups. A unitary state aiming at the creation of a single "Ghanaian" culture could become a feasible goal.

It seemed at first that this struggle could itself become the basis for a true party system and a liberal constitutional regime, which would be far less severely plagued by regional politics and fissiparous tendencies than Nigeria. The majority party, the Convention Peoples' Party (CPP) led by Kwame Nkrumah, was more truly national than any Nigerian party, and had branches and strong support in every area except the far north—and even there was not without some influence. The opposition, it was true, was based on a somewhat motley collection of local groups—the National Liberation Movement in Ashanti, the Northern Peoples' Party in the North, and Ga and Ewe movements—but even these came together in November 1957 (shortly after independence) to form the United Party (UP) as an official opposition. It might have seemed to many at that time that Ghanaian politics were clarifying themselves into a pattern in which a national radical socialist party, the CPP as the ruling government, was facing up to a national conservative party, the UP, in opposition. Both sides, immediately before independence, had shown tolerance and responsibility, the opposition by dropping the demand for federation, and the CPP by agreeing to set up interim regional assemblies within the unitary state, with entrenched clauses in the constitution giving security to minority rights and interests. Nkrumah himself had extolled the virtues of liberal democracy on the eve of independence.

However, this was not to be. Far from developing upon liberal lines, the newly independent state moved, gradually but steadily, along a course which dismantled all the safeguards in the constitution one by one, intimidated the opposition by arbitrary arrests, developed a thesis which equated the ruling party with the state, reshaped farmers', workers', and consumers' associations along fascist lines as organs of the party and the state, and transformed the parliamentary regime of 1957 into a corporate state led by an Heroic Leader.

Two main arguments have been advanced by both Nkrumah and his critics to advocate the inevitability of this development. The first is pragmatic: that the situation of a newly independent African state is essentially one of permanent crisis, threatened from within by "tribalism" and disunity and from without by "neocolonialism."

This situation is compared to that of a state at war, when individual liberties have to be suspended for the duration of the emergency. Opposition to the state in these conditions is not legitimate but treasonable. The second argument is more subtle, and couched in terms of African nationalism. It asserts that single-party rule is the "natural form" of African society, which is corporate and communal, and that opposing political parties are a European importation unsuited to African conditions, where organized opposition to the ruler in precolonial times was unknown. Discussion of a loyal kind would take place before decisions were taken, but these would be within the single community structure, and after decisions were made they were not questioned. The single party which is the state can fulfill this traditional function: discussion before decision will occur within it, for it represents the whole community.

Of the two arguments the first is nearer to the truth, for Ghana, like Nigeria, was faced, although on a lesser scale, with regional and "tribal" pressures which threatened, or appeared to threaten, the state. Whether these could be compared to a wartime situation is open to doubt, particularly when one notes that Nigeria, with much more dangerous forces of regional separatism, managed for so long to contain them without single party rule or dictatorship. It is difficult to avoid dismissing the second argument as pure nonsense, for the CPP has shown no disposition to look with favor on traditional African political institutions, which are alien to its aims and objectives. The argument is particularly absurd when applied to Akan institutions, which were especially remarkable for the way in which opposition could be expressed to the rulers, who could be and were frequently "destooled" (dethroned) for unconstitutional or unpopular acts.

The emergence of dictatorship in Ghana is not, therefore, explained either by the nature of the crises which faced the country after 1957, or by the idea of an inevitable assertion of "African-ness" on political institutions. The explanation lies much more in the nature of the CPP as a political movement. The composition of the CPP shows striking similarities with fascist movements in Europe and Latin America. Like them it attracted few intellectuals or aristocrats, except for a small number of leaders. Its mass support was composed of underprivileged elements, often suffering a sense of economic grievance, backed by a feeling of lack of status and discrimination against them, which was easy to blame on foreigners. In Ghana these were the growing number of elementary-school-leavers, literate people whose hopes of advancement were frustrated by lack of opportunities for higher education and limited scope for employment as skilled workers in a backward economy. Such people naturally resented the superior attitudes of the intellectuals and chiefs, and responded to the CPP gospel that unity and self-government would rid the country of foreign oppression and poverty. Few in the CPP could be expected to absorb the sophisticated tolerance and liberalism of highly educated opposition leaders like Busia or Danquah, and the experience of the colonial period had given no training to the masses in liberal self-government. The CPP was composed of simple people who wanted to be "on the move" to the "promised land." The philosophical meanderings of silver-tongued lawyers counseling caution and moderation seemed merely obstruction to them. They wanted strong leadership and a firm goal, and Kwame Nkrumah was prepared to give it.

It can be argued that the attitudes of rank-and-file membership in the southern political parties in Nigeria were much the same, as indeed they were. But in Nigeria no single party could bid for complete dominance, and the party leaders' task after 1960 was to pass down the party structure the message of the complex political realities in Nigeria. Nor in Nigeria was there the divorce between the intellectual leaders and the masses which had occurred in the CPP. Nkrumah after independence faced no such limitations on his personal will, he was undisputed leader of a dominant united party with mass support, whose members cared little about constitutional forms. It was really up to him to determine the future pattern of political life. Had he been a man to whom a liberal democratic way of life had seemed important he could have led the CPP along such paths.

However, he was not such a man. He showed no reluctance to don the mantle of the Heroic Leader and made no attempt to check the growth of the cult of his own personality. His face appeared on Ghana's coins and stamps, his statue immodestly graced the public squares, and the party press and literature praised him in ever more effusive sycophancy like some late-Roman Caesar. Such outward show corresponded to more serious political steps designed, first, to destroy all opposition and, second, to enshrine permanently in constitutional form the dominance of the party and its leader.

If there was little in the nature of the CPP or in the character of its leader to prevent dictatorship, the opposition must also share the responsibility. Whether a more responsible opposition would have moderated the CPP policies is doubtful, but the behavior of the opposition lent force to the argument that an "emergency" situation existed, and that the object of opposition was to destroy the unity of the country. The opposition gave public sympathy and support to the revolt of certain Ewe villages demanding unification with Togoland in 1957, and later in that year it favored the Ga Shifimo Kpee, formed in Accra to advocate Ga interests. In 1958 the general secretary of the opposition parties, R. R. Amponsah, became involved in a ludicrous plot, involving his purchase of canes, badges, and belts from a military outfitter in London. These affairs met with an appropriate response by the government. In August 1957 a Deportation Act was passed, in December an Emergency Powers Act, and after the Amponsah affair a Preventive Detention Act of July 1958 allowed the government to imprison without trial any person suspected of activities prejudicial to state security. By November 1958 38 members of the opposition had been detained.

At the same time the CPP was quick to destroy the constitutional checks on its power after independence. In December 1957 all regional, tribal, or religious parties were forbidden, and this was followed by a full-scale attack on the chiefs who were sympathetic to the opposition. These were downgraded in status, while CPP chiefs were upgraded, and several were destooled and replaced by CPP nominees. Every chief in Ashanti who had supported the National Liberation Movement was removed except the asantehene (King of Ashanti) himself. Regional Commissioners were appointed, all of them CPP members. Finally, in 1958, the Regional Assemblies were established with only advisory powers; the elections to them were boycotted by the opposition with the result that all five assemblies fell under CPP control. The Assemblies met briefly in September 1958 only to approve their own abolition, which was passed through Parliament in 1959 with the required two-thirds majority.

In 1959 the CPP began openly to assert its claims to a one-party state. In June Nkrumah announced at a party rally ". . . the Convention People's Party is Ghana." By this time the framework for the corporate state had been laid down. The Trade Union Council had been reorganized by the Industrial Relations Act of 1958, the cooperative movement had been organized under the National Cooperative Council, and a Ghana Farmers' Council set up as the sole representative body for farmers. All of these bodies became CPP-controlled.

In 1960 came the open establishment of a new Constitution designed to give Nkrumah a commanding position in the state. Parliamentary government was substantially altered by the creation of a Presidential system, in which Nkrumah was appointed First President (subsequent presidents were to be elected by Parliament) with powers to legislate without Parliament. Ministers were no longer to be responsible to Parliament. The new constitution was submitted to a referendum of the electors at the same time as they were asked to elect Nkrumah First President. The election and referendum was remarkable as the first example in Ghana of the government using its power to affect the result. Danquah, the opposition's candidate, was not allowed time on the Ghana radio, and when the first stage of polling in Accra, watched closely by foreign observers and journalists, showed massive abstentions and with Danquah obtaining a third of the 45 per cent of electors who voted, the Government "made sure" that this fiasco was not repeated in the interior, where polling took place later. Here the results showed 80 per cent polls, and even more than 90 per cent in some cases. Some results, especially in the opposition strongholds in Ashanti, were ridiculous. In Atwima Nwabiagya, for instance, where the CPP in the election of 1956 obtained only 1,390 votes to the opposition's 8,334 in a 70 per cent poll, the result in 1960 in a 90 per cent poll gave the CPP over 20,000 votes to the opposition's 155!

After 1960 Ghana was for all practical purposes, though not officially, a single-party state. This being so, the focus of political conflict fell on the party itself, which by 1961 had become a group of warring factions. There followed a series of purges and dismissals carried out by Nkrumah himself, played out against ever-increasing violence. In 1962 a bomb was thrown near Nkrumah's automobile, and ministers traveling in the party who were suspiciously far away were arrested. A Special Court was set up to try them, under the presidency of the Chief Justice, Sir Arku Korsah. In December the court acquitted the three accused ex-ministers. Two days later Nkrumah dismissed the Chief Justice. The National Assembly was called into special session and passed a new act which permitted Nkrumah to quash the Court's verdict. Shortly afterwards it was announced that early in 1964 a referendum would be held on two constitutional amendments giving the President the power to dismiss any High Court Judge "at any time for reasons which appear to him sufficient" and declaring that "there will be only one national party in Ghana [and] that the one national party shall be the Convention People's Party." Before the referendum was held a police constable fired five ineffective shots at Nkrumah inside his headquarters at Flagstaff House; there followed more arrests and six of the faculty of the University of Ghana were deported.

The results of the plebiscite on the two constitutional amendments held early in 1964 were even more absurd than the Ashanti results of 1960. It was claimed that 92.8 per cent of the whole national electorate had voted, 2,773,920 for, and 2,452 against the amendments!

The final culmination of this process was seen in the "general election" of June 1965, when all the parliamentary candidates were "returned unopposed" without a single exception, and the electors were not even given the opportunity of spoiling their ballot papers, for no polling at all took place, and the list of "elected" candidates was simply announced by the government. The increasingly totalitarian nature of Nkrumah's regime may have been intensified by economic and international frustrations. It was perhaps natural that Ghana, as the first tropical African colony to secure independence, should initially have played a role in international affairs which exaggerated Ghana's real power and influence. Nkrumah had a long association with pan-African ideas, first in his student days in the U.S.A. when he fell under the influence of Marcus Garvey's "Back to Africa" movement and later in London. The CPP manifesto and the Constitution of 1960 both enshrined the goal of African unity. In November 1958 Ghana and the ex-French territory of Guinea formed a symbolic "union" open to all African states, which Mali joined in 1960. In 1958 the first conference of independent African states was held in Accra. But with the emergence of many more independent African states Nkrumah's leadership waned. Some of the new states were much larger than Ghana and had acute problems of internal unity which seemed to them more pressing than African unity. These problems often made them more conservative and more friendly to their ex-colonial masters, who could provide them with administrators, technicians, and economic and military aid. This was especially the case with Nigeria, which, as the largest African state, naturally felt a claim to leadership, and with the ex-French colonies who kept many links with France. With the independence of these groups after 1960 Nkrumah was increasingly eclipsed. In January 1962 when 20 independent African states met in Lagos, Ghana and the "radicals" of the "Casablanca group" refused to attend. In May 1963 at the Addis Ababa conference of all 32 independent African States, Nkrumah's isolation was highlighted when he personally put forward an utterly unrealistic scheme for a Union of African States, with a common currency, banking system, defense, citizenship, and foreign policy. He found himself in a minority of one, his proposals were ignored, and when the conference went on to set up a Liberation Committee to assist nationalists in the remaining colonial areas and in South Africa, Ghana was excluded.

Even more serious were the economic difficulties which began to face the regime after 1961. These were not primarily of the government's making, but stemmed from world conditions. Ghana's economy is highly dependent on the world price of cocoa, the chief export crop. Since the CPP first gained power in 1951 there have, of course, been fluctuations and occasional falls in the cocoa price, but on the whole the price rose considerably between 1951 and 1958. This allowed the general standard of living to rise, while at the same time surpluses, along with assistance from foreign aid, could be used for development. Large and important development projects were begun such as the huge Volta scheme, designed to harness massive hydro electric power to make the economic extraction of Ghana's bauxite deposits possible, and to set up aluminum smelting, as well as many other industrial projects. The effect will be to make Ghana the first tropical African state to break away from almost complete dependence on primary agricultural production. Besides the Volta scheme, much development took place in road-building, primary education was established on a massive scale, and millions were invested in the construction of artificial harbors at Tema and Takoradi.

In 1959, however, the cocoa price fell sharply from £352 to £285 per ton. In 1960 it was down to £225 a ton, and in 1961 it fell to £177 a ton. The effect was very serious: it cut down purchasing power at home at a time when the prices of imported goods were rising, and presented the state with acute balance-of-payments difficulties, threatening the whole development plan. In addition the drop in purchasing power naturally cut down the revenues of the state. Popular discontent began to show itself, and there were strikes and labor difficulties. Because the fall in cocoa prices was produced by world factors outside the Ghana government's control, it was natural that it should reinforce Nkrumah's ideological stand on pan-Africanism and neocolonialism: the fall in the cocoa price was portrayed as a neocolonialist plot on the part of rich imperialistic powers to stifle Ghana's development. The Ghana government refused to respond by reducing government expenditure and slowing down development, and instead tried to deal with the balance of payments by strict currency control. In December 1964, after an agreement with Nigeria, Brazil, the Ivory Coast, the Cameroons, and Togo, Ghana began burning cocoa in order to try to raise the price to £190 a ton. Meanwhile the budget for 1965 provided for further large spending up to £250 million, although it was difficult to see how revenue could have exceeded £130 million for the year. Previous budget deficits had already reduced the reserves to £25 million by February 1965, while the obligations of future commitments for development plans were £150 million. In February 1965 the international banks refused to extend any further cover for imports or development projects, and serious shortages of imported goods had already become acute. At present Ghana, in effect, faces imminent financial collapse. Just how this will affect Nkrumah's regime remains to be seen.

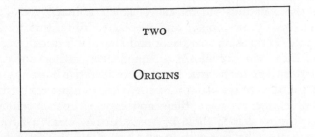

TWO

ORIGINS

The Emergence of the Negro

It is now virtually certain, thanks to recent archaeological discoveries, that man originated in Africa. Some two million years ago, at Olduvai Gorge in Tanzania, manlike creatures (hominids) made the first steps to differentiate themselves from beasts by using stones, sticks, and bones as simple tools which they held in their hands. Somewhat later they began to shape these materials deliberately for useful purposes, and became tool-makers. As yet these creatures were not true men (*homo sapiens*), for although they were bipeds, with intelligence enough to take this revolutionary step and hands dexterous enough to contain the skill, their short stature, smaller brains, and different jaw and teeth patterns made them zoologically distinct from true man. Within a few hundred thousand years several types of tool-making hominids were scattered throughout Africa, and their sites have been found in Algeria and Morocco, in South Africa, and around Lake Chad on the borders of Nigeria.

The climate of Africa was significantly different in prehistoric times. Most of southern Ghana and Nigeria were covered, as today, with tropical forest which formed the western arms of the great Congo basin forest. The hominids avoided the forest because their tools were not sufficiently developed to tame it and because they had not yet discovered how to use fire. Living by the hunting of animals, they ranged the broad savannah which covered most of Africa, including the Sahara, which at that time was not desert and enjoyed reasonable rainfall.

Sometime after 1,000,000 B.C. a new and important refinement of toolmaking, produced by the attachment of larger sharpened stones

33

at right angles to a wooden shaft, created the handaxe. This tool allowed the hominids to kill much larger animals, including the earliest forms of ox, giraffe, and elephant. With this increase in food supply, population increased, and the handaxe cultures spread outside Africa into Europe, Asia Minor, and India. Tools were accumulated and groups became larger for cooperative hunting.

With the separation of groups, specialized cultures suited to different environments made their appearance, distinct enough for archaeologists to denote them by specialized names. In Africa after 500,000 B.C. the Chellean culture gave way about 250,000 B.C. to the Acheulian, both of these being essentially cultures of the savannah.

At the end of the Acheulian period, about 50,000 B.C., our ancestors in Africa began to use fire. This development made it possible to move into the rain forest area, where a new culture—the Sangoan—emerged, characterized by the heavier chopping tools needed in the forest, and a large range of woodworking stone tools. The Sangoan settlements were usually centered in caves and rock shelters, these settlements always showing the use of fire pits.

From this time forward it is possible to mark distinct regional cultures in Africa, produced by environmental differences, separate tool-making techniques, and the effects of separation through long periods of time. While the Sangoan people covered most of West Africa, both forest and savannah, they were absent from North Africa, where a distinct hominid creature—the Neanderthal—who may have originated in Europe, produced the Levallous-Mousterian culture.

At the beginning of the middle stone age, around 35,000 B.C., true man (*homo sapiens*) made his appearance both in Africa and Europe. His stone-working techniques were much more refined and complex, and his control of the environment correspondingly greater. In Africa the middle-stone-age cultures show two broad variations, though it would be a mistake to presume that this represented as yet any racial formation within the family of *homo sapiens*. The basic difference between these two cultures was in their tool complement, which in turn reflected the demands of their differing environments. Most of southern and eastern Africa were covered by the Stillbay culture, where projectile tools were important for hunting in more open country, while in the Congo and West African forest the middle-stone-age cultures conserved the heavy choppers and developed stabbing tools more appropriate to the forest conditions. In both areas, however, as in middle-stone-age cultures throughout the world, this period saw the emergence of a spiritual, religious, and artistic aspect to life, evidenced in the ritual of burials and in rock paintings.

Between 10,000 and 8,000 B.C. there is evidence that the races of man had begun to emerge. In North Africa we know that two distinct immigrations of Caucasoids occurred which laid the basis for the creation of the "Proto-Hamitic" race, bearing linguistic relationships with Semitic languages of the Middle East. The "Mongol" race and its offshoots was also well established by this time in Asia. In South and East Africa the so-called "Bushmen" stock with its characteristic Khoisian languages was also in being. The language characteristics of the races were obviously produced by development after separation, but just how the minor physical differences occurred remains obscure. Some would argue that differences of average size, head shapes, hair formation, and eyelids occurred by mutation in response to environmental demands. Others assert that racial differences occurred by interbreeding of early *homo sapiens* with different forms of hominids. The question of how skin color became a mark of racial difference is probably a distinct one, for all races have the mechanism of skin pigmentation. It would seem that a deep brown skin color is the natural one of *homo sapiens*, and that the "white" races (including the Mongols) have a physical deficiency which prevents the skin pigmentation process from operating, except partially under the stimulus of ultraviolet light. Skin color differentiation, therefore, probably occurred *after* the formation of races. The inability to pigment the skin may in fact be akin to a hereditary disease which at some time swept the Caucasoid and Mongol races.

The origin of the Negro race, however, remains something of a mystery. Such evidence as exists would seem to indicate that the Negro arrived late on the scene in Africa, after the major races were well established. Whether this was because the Negro was the last of the major races to evolve, or whether he evolved earlier somewhere in Asia and migrated to Africa later, thus only appearing to be a late evolution, remains in doubt. The peoples of Polynesia and

Melanesia, as well as the aboriginal inhabitants of India, are remarkably like the African Negro physically, and yet their languages bear no relationship to his. This might indicate a remote common origin elsewhere, perhaps in Asia Minor. Negroes themselves have remarkably consistent legends of their origins in the Middle East—some even specify Arabia—but the modern influence of Islam may have simply created prestige legends with no historical basis. Whatever his remote origins, the first real archaeological evidence of the Negro is from the Sahara in the period before it became desert. Rock paintings from Saharan caves clearly show a Negroid people, subsisting from the hunting of characteristic savannah animals, giraffe and elephant among them. Archaeological evidence suggests that the Negro in his earliest stage was especially remarkable as a fisherman in the lakes and rivers which then existed in the Sahara. This is important as showing an early cultural advance by the Negroes, a first step which was to lead to their eventual conquest of almost the whole continent south of the Sahara; for fishing, while it was still in a sense a hunting economy, allowed permanent settlement and village life to begin. Once permanent settlement occurred the beginning of agriculture was much more likely, as villagers began to notice the effects of the seasons upon wild vegetation and the improved quality of wild plants accidentally growing in manure-rich rubbish dumps.

The Negro is in fact characterized in early African history as the bringer of the agricultural revolution. It was his adoption of an agricultural way of life which allowed the race to grow much faster than the Bushmen or pygmy people, and this growth of population produced a Negro bursting-forth, lasting for several thousand years, which took him as a conqueror over every part of Africa south of the Sahara. Scholars disagree as to the process by which the Negro originally became agricultural. Most are agreed, however, that the Negro adopted agriculture in West Africa at roughly the same time as the Sahara began to dry up and be formed into a desert, around 4,000 B.C. The Negro populations of the Sahara were therefore forced to move south in search of water and fishing places. It was natural that the rivers of the savannah region, and especially the upper Niger, should have become foci for further advance. Where scholars disagree is on whether the transition to agriculture was an independent Negro invention or whether it was adopted by import-

ing the technique from outside. G. P. Murdoch (see the SUGGESTED
READINGS in the back of this volume) has argued that the Negroes
independently invented agriculture on the upper Niger and spread
the technique throughout the western Sudan between 5,000 and
4,000 B.C. His ideas have failed to win general acceptance, and much
of his botanical evidence has been challenged by those who argue
that the Negro adopted agriculture by borrowing from Egypt, by a
slow process of diffusion through the eastern Sudan and across the
savannah belt to the west. But whether the technique was borrowed
or not, the agricultural complex was indigenous, i.e., the Negroes
did not take over Egyptian crops and plants, for these, like barley,
were not suitable for the savannah area. Instead they ennobled local
grasses to produce millets and sorghum, as well as local pulses, fruit,
nuts, and perhaps an indigenous form of cotton. Such a development
was truly revolutionary, for it represented a major step in dominating
the environment. By creating his own food supply instead of being
dependent on the luck of hunting, the Negro was able to begin
population expansion and set up agriculture throughout the western
Sudan, as a springboard for the colonization of the forest zone.

Agricultural revolutions elsewhere—in the Mesopotamian area,
Jordan, or Egypt, for instance—led to the development of complex
civilizations. In West Africa this development was much slower,
primarily because the agricultural revolution was achieved with
greater ease in an environment which did not demand a complex
political structure. In Egypt, for instance, agriculture was impossible
without the imposition of a number of social controls on the use
of the Nile waters, and the state developed primarily as an organ for
irrigation. The needs of irrigation led in turn to studies of the
calendar and seasons, and to the creation of a priestly cult. Egypt
also had the advantage of constant contact and borrowing through
routes across the Mediterranean and the Sinai peninsula with the
other civilizations of Southwest Asia. In West Africa irrigation was
not important, and agriculture could be organized by village political
units; also, the area of savannah agriculture had no seacoast and no
easy means of contact for cross-fertilization with other civilizations.

Nevertheless the basis for a civilization, though much more slowly
and less spectacularly, was being laid down after 2,000 B.C. by the
creation in very difficult geographical circumstances of contacts with

the outside world. As the Sahara dried up, the Berbers (a Caucasian people who had colonized North Africa) began building trade contacts across the desert, bringing the agricultural complex which they had learned from Egypt to the remaining Negroes of the Sahara, who used agriculture to build the chains of oases around what was left of the water resources in the desert. These Negro oases formed the steppingstones for Berber traders to enter the northern fringes of the savannah. These northern-savannah Negroes absorbed some Egyptian agricultural techniques and plants from the Berbers, who may also have introduced the domestication of cattle (which were not milked) into the western Sudan. At the same time there were contacts eastward with the eastern Sudan, from whom animals and Ethiopian plants may have been obtained.

The demands of trade and the stimulus of outside contact undoubtedly laid the basis for a more complex political structure and the beginnings of urban civilization, which probably began on the edges of the desert. As yet almost nothing is known of these in the pre-Christian era. The earliest culture of which we have detailed archaeological evidence comes from further south, where tin-mining operations on the Jos plateau in Nigeria began the discovery of the Nok culture.

The Nok culture spanned most of the first millennium B.C. from about 900 B.C. until about A.D. 200. What we know of the culture is based on the remarkable terra cotta sculpture which it produced, and on stool tools and jewelry found in excavations. These show that the Nok people built a society of considerable complexity, in which specialist crafts and wealth had made their appearance. Beads of tin and quartz were manufactured for adornment, and all artistic activity had reached a high level of attainment. The terra cotta sculptures depict several varieties of animals, but above all they concentrate on the human face and head. It is very likely that such artistic activity was prompted by religion, that the animal-figures may have had religious meanings now lost to us, and that the human figures were connected with a cult of ancestors. Such activities show that agricultural production had reached a point where surpluses were large enough to provide for a craftsman and artist class, and probably for a priesthood also. It is safe to assume that the complexity of society demanded also some sophistication in the political structure.

The Nok culture of the Jos plateau was also a springboard for Negro advance into the forest areas. The later archaeological evidence at Nok shows that it was the scene of another revolution in the life of the Negro which took place at about the time of Christ. This was the introduction of iron-working. The importance of this technique can hardly be exaggerated; it was to make the Negro dominant both economically and militarily in most of tropical Africa for the next fifteen hundred years. Iron tools made it possible for the Negro to produce a new agricultural system and set of crops with which to colonize the tropical forest. Iron weapons made it certain that the Negro could conquer and absorb the aboriginal pygmy and bush stocks of stone-age people who might resist him. Iron tools also increased the agricultural production of the nuclear areas such as the Nok area, thus increasing population even further and providing the manpower for expansion.

The agricultural crops of the savannah and plateau were in no way suitable for the forest area, so that the colonization of the forest needed more than simply iron tools. Suitable crops were in fact provided by Southeast Asian food crops, especially the banana and the Asian yam, brought first to Madagascar by Indonesian settlers after 1,000 B.C. These plants crossed Africa and reached West Africa just at the time of the introduction of iron. The yam was to become the staple crop of the West African forest.

The Nok culture could hardly have been the sole diffusion point of this Negro conquest of the forest, even in Nigeria alone. Further west and in Ghana the original Negro colonists of the forest areas may have come from other nuclear centers, though linguistic evidence still would indicate that they came from somewhere in northern Nigeria. Systematic archaeological survey would probably reveal a number of early iron-smelting centers in addition to Nok along the savannah belt. However, the Nok culture clearly possessed a special significance as a diffusion center, for the artistic styles of the Nok terra cottas emerge centuries later in terra cotta and brass sculpture of the Yoruba. Linguistic evidence also suggests that the Jos plateau language pattern may comprise present descendants of languages which were the ancient prototypes from which most southern Nigerian languages could have developed.

However, the story of the Negro conquest of the forest is by no means clear, and much research is needed before even the main lines of this major historical theme can be settled. The above account—of the diffusion of Negro agricultural techniques and peoples southward from the savannah to tame the forest with iron tools planting Indonesian crops—is the generally accepted hypothesis. It is, however, undermined by two considerations. The first is linguistic. Although the languages of southern Nigeria and southern Ghana all belong to the same major family (the Niger-Congo family), and although nearly all can be further classified into two subfamilies—the Kwa subfamily (which includes Ibo, Yoruba, and Twi) and the Bantoid subfamily (which includes Efik, Ibibio, and languages of the Jos plateau)—nevertheless the languages within these subfamilies are distinct and differ very greatly, some so radically that it is hardly feasible that they could have stemmed from the same parent language less than three or four thousand years ago. Yet we know that the use of iron and the introduction of the Indonesian forest food crops occurred only about two thousand years ago. The second consideration which undermines the generally accepted hypothesis is the existence of the Guinea yam. This root plant, akin to the Asian yam which is now the staple, is known to be indigenous to West Africa and to the forest region. It is therefore possible that agriculture existed in the forest area *before* the introduction of the Indonesian crops.

Another hypothesis may therefore be suggested, i.e., that Negroes from the savannah area began to colonize the forest before the iron age, moving there between 4,000 and 3,000 B.C. with stone tools and developing agriculture based on the Guinea yam. With iron technology further groups of Negroes came from the north in the first millennium A.D., adopting the Indonesian plants which the local people might already have begun using. But these newcomers were a minority group, hence their languages did not replace those of the existing communities, which had developed as distinct tongues after one or two thousand years of separation from common original parents. The newcomers, equipped with iron, would easily conquer the majority, but they would tend to monopolize iron technology and surround it with frightening magical and religious associations. Hence blacksmiths, until quite recently, were often organized in tight, exclusive guilds and were thought to have magical powers, and hence the common legends that the founders of some southern states were blacksmiths. The original Negroes were probably organized on a simple communal pattern in village groups, but the new Negro invaders with their iron weapons would be able to organize larger units, and would naturally place themselves in positions of authority—hence kingship and chieftainship and true states began to emerge. The new rulers would naturally impose their own ideology and religion upon the masses and surround their authority with religious and magical associations; they would also try to wipe out previous folk legends and build new historical myths which placed the foundation of the state and society at the time of their own coming. But they would not be able to change the old languages, which would hold their ground by sheer weight of the numbers who spoke them. Such a hypothesis would also explain the absence of any real evidence of an aboriginal population in southern Ghana or southern Nigeria. If the Negro conquest and colonization was less than two thousand years ago some traces of primitive stone-age pre-agricultural peoples, who would not be Negro, should remain. In the Congo area and southern Africa, which were conquered by Bantu Negroes after the time of Christ, the aboriginal pygmy and Bushman groups still exist. In West Africa there are legends of "little people," but so are there in Ireland. If the assumption is made of a stone-age Negro settlement two or three millennia before the iron-age conquest by Negro minorities, however, the absence of any trace of aborigines is explained.

The Creation of States

The conquest of the forest areas by iron-using Negro groups from the north in the early centuries after Christ was the result of population growth made possible by the effect of iron tools on the savannah agricultural communities. This population growth was naturally felt first in the savannah areas, and it was to have political consequences there. Events in North Africa and the Sahara desert also helped to shape these developments. As the population and wealth of the savannah areas increased, so also did trade across the Sahara, first developed by the Berbers. When North Africa witnessed the development of the Phoenician colony of Carthage, little was done to disturb the Berbers in their control of the hinterland trade routes (though the Carthaginians attempted to bypass them by opening direct sea communications around the West African coast). When Carthage fell to Roman power the Romans continued to leave the trans-Saharan trade in Berber hands. The trade seems to have developed steadily, the main exports of the savannah being gold, kola nuts, ivory, and slaves, in return for salt, cloth, beads, and horses. As routes were defined, naturally regular market places were established, and political regulations had to be made for them. Considerable urban centers began to arise at the southern end of the trade routes, and these began to develop as the capitals of the surrounding areas.

Unfortunately the earliest detailed picture of the savannah area comes to us only when literate Muslims began traveling there and writing descriptions at the end of the first millennium A.D., by which time the state systems of the savannah were well established. These descriptions reveal that the political institutions of these states had much in common, and that the spirit of their political philosophy was so little related to Islam that their origins must lie well before the beginnings of Muslim influence in West Africa. The characteristic institution of these states was divine kingship, or what some writers have called "African despotism." The king was regarded as being quite distinct from normal humans and as being in personal contact with God or with the forces of nature. Elaborate procedures were followed to hide his humanity; not even the most intimate of his courtiers were allowed to see him eat or drink, and his food was smuggled into his presence. His face was never seen by his people, and he spoke only from behind a screen or curtain. Often his feet were not permitted to touch the ground, and his health was thought to symbolize the health of the state. He was thus never permitted to die of illness or old age, but poisoned or made to commit ritual suicide. At his death human sacrifices were made.

The state itself was highly bureaucratic and not feudal in structure. Theoretically the king was absolute ruler with complete power. He ruled not through a territorial aristocracy but through titled courtiers who served as his ministers in the capital and often also as governors of provinces at the same time. In all these states special pre-eminence was given to the queen-mother, queen-sister and queen-consort, who sometimes shared the function of determining the succession to the throne.

The prevalence of these institutions was remarkable, and the divine kingship of this pattern was found in large empires ruling over a million or more people, and also in petty states which were little more than glorified villages. Such states spanned across formidable language barriers, and indeed they were not confined to West Africa at all, but were found in the eastern Sudan, East Africa and even in the Rhodesias. Some historians have maintained, basing their argument upon legends of "white" men as the first kings of the earliest empires, that they were the result of the infiltration of Jews and Berbers who established themselves as rulers over the Negroes. By the time of the Arab writers, however, there is no trace of anything other than Negro rulers, and the divine-kingship pattern was just as strong, and indeed was to persist and spread as a characteristic African system of kingship. A much more likely hypothesis is that this pattern of divine kingship represented influence—transmitted indirectly—from ancient Egypt. The divine kingship of African states corresponds remarkably to the divine position of the Pharaohs, and many of the taboos surrounding the king were identical with those of ancient Egypt. The position of the queen-sister in Egypt is also one which seems to have been transferred to the queen-mother in African states (where the African social systems forbade the marriage of brother and sister as practiced by the Egyptian royals).

Just how this Egyptian influence was transmitted is still a matter of speculation. The most probable explanation is that it came by way of the Negro states of the upper Nile Valley, which developed divine monarchies closely patterned on their northern Egyptian neighbors and at one time conquered Egypt. The diffusion center may have been Meroe, the great iron-producing settlement on the upper Nile. It may well be that ideas of divine kingship and iron weapons left Meroe together, in the hands of small bands of Negro adventurers or refugees, who used both to set themselves up as rulers further west, and gradually spread across to the Atlantic along the savannah belt. On the other hand the Negroes of the Sahara may have played an important role. These, the rump of those who

had not fled south to begin the agricultural revolution thousands of
years earlier, were rapidly finding themselves reduced to servile
status by the Berbers of North Africa, who wished to dominate the
oases on the trade routes to the south. Groups of Sahara Negroes
who had had contact with Egyptian civilization across the Sahara
may have fled southwards after A.D. 100 and established divine kingships in the savannah area.

Whatever the explanation of origins, the story of the western
savannah areas from this time until the colonial occupation is one
of the rise and fall of large empires of the divine-monarchy pattern,
all of which show a definite economic strategy of attempting to
control the sources of gold production on the upper Niger valley
and a desire to control the southern termini of the trade routes to
the north. At the same time smaller states, often much less ambitious, existed side by side with them, operating on the same pattern
of divine kingship, sometimes falling under the temporary domination of a larger empire, but often having a much longer continuous
history than the great empires. The earliest of the great empires
was Ghana, a state which may have originated as early as the
fourth century A.D., and which was centered on the large area
north of the watersheds of the Senegal and Niger rivers. It thus has
no historical connection with modern Ghana, whose nationalist
politicians adopted the name as a symbolic assertion of African-ness.
Old Ghana was conquered by the Almoravid Muslims of North
Africa in the eleventh century, but upon its ruins new Negro empires were built, of which the first was Mali, a giant state which
lasted until the coming of the Europeans and sent an embassy to
Portugal; then came Songhai, which dominated practically the whole
of the upper Niger from Senegal to northern Nigeria in the sixteenth
century.

Neither northern Ghana nor northern Nigeria, however, were
scenes of empire-building on this scale.

With regard to the northern area of Ghana, we know very little
of the history of the people before A.D. 1400. The area was not one
which was of great importance in the trade patterns created by the
trans-Saharan routes; thus there is little evidence from early Muslim
travelers, and the traditions of the people have been destroyed or
absorbed by conquering peoples after 1400. What we do know is

that before 1400 the northern peoples spoke the same languages of
the Voltaic subfamily which they speak today, and that they were
organized under totemic clans under divine priest-kings, with a
system of inheritance through the deceased's sister's son. The priest-
kings were seen as arbiters between man and nature, and their
function seems principally to have been that of preventing divine
anger by making sacrifices when taboos, such as the spilling of blood
upon the soil, were offended. Outside connections at this time seem
to have been mainly with the south. A trade existed with the
coastal areas for salt, and kola nuts were imported from the forest
region for local use and for re-export northwards, where they would
eventually find their way over the Saharan routes through various
middlemen.

The historical evidence for the early development of states in
northern Nigeria is very much richer, largely because of its greater
importance as a terminus of the trans-Saharan trade, which attracted
the attention of Arab geographers and travelers. An earlier penetration of Islam into the area also created a local literature which
did much to preserve local traditions. The contrast, however, is not
merely one of evidence, for northern Nigeria was in fact a cultural
crossroads, where the interaction of competing influences produced
a more complex situation. In the first millennium after Christ northern Nigeria was a natural meeting point of influences—from the
east as a result of the breakup of the ancient Egyptian civilization
and the rise of the Negro civilizations of the Nile valley centered on
Meroe with its iron technology; and from the north, where suc-
cessive invasions of North Africa, which culminated in its conquest
by Arabs after the time of Muhamed, in turn intensified Berber
pressures on the Negroes of the Sahara and continued their tendency
to migrate southwards.

The earliest states in northern Nigeria were probably founded by
Negro migrants from the northeast, and what we know of their institutions strongly suggests that they were founded by immigrants
who had been closely if indirectly influenced by the ideas of kingship in the Negro kingdoms of Meroe and Kush in the Nile valley.
They may also have been able to establish their authority over the
indigenous Negro agriculturalists by the use of iron weapons. The
states which they founded were centered on walled capital cities,

and ruled over by divine kings of the pattern described earlier. This movement occurred sometime before the sixth century after Christ.

In the seventh and eighth centuries the state structure was affected by the intrusion of non-Negroes. These were the Zaghawa, a Berber people, pushed southward by the Arab invasions of North Africa. In 667 a group of Zaghawa conquered Fezzan, at that time a Negro state on the fringe of the Sahara immediately north of Lake Chad. In material culture the Zaghawa, being a pastoral people, were less developed than the Negroes whose lands they intruded. Their political organization, however, was tighter and more disciplined, they were more mobile, and their men fought on horseback. The newcomers may originally have penetrated peacefully, but by the eighth century they had seized political power from the Negroes and had begun to use their cavalry to weld together a larger state unit. Its nucleus lay to the east of Lake Chad, and it was to become the empire of Kanem-Bornu, a state with a thousand years of continuous history under a single dynasty of rulers.

Despite their political superiority over the Negroes, however, the Zaghawa were themselves rapidly assimilated by Negro culture. As they settled down in walled cities as rulers, their pastoral institutions evaporated, they intermarried with influential Negro families, and the kingship developed exactly along the lines of a typical Negro kingdom. The king (mai) was a divine person, worshipped by his subjects, who regarded him as the origin of life and death, and who believed that he never consumed food. The queen-mother possessed great influence, and the elaborate court ritual was devised to conceal from the populace the king's mortality and humanity. The court was the center of a bureaucratic regime of councillors and provincial governors. Within a short time there was hardly a trace of Berber influence, and by the twelfth century the kings were regarded by Arab travelers as "pure" Negroes.

The growth of this empire, and its longevity, were closely connected with its strategic position. It lay at the southern end of the most easterly of the trade routes from North to West Africa, which started from Tripoli, where goods from the Mediterranean and Near East were dispatched via Murzuk and Bilma to Kanem-Bornu. Here the caravans ended their journey, selling their beads, glassware, salt, swords and chainmail, cloths and lightweight manufactured goods of all kinds, and taking in exchange ivory, gold, ostrich feathers, ebony, kola nuts, and slaves. The Kanem merchants in turn distributed the imports southward and westward.

After the time of Muhamed, with the blossoming of medieval Arab civilization in North Africa, the Arabs increasingly dominated the trans-Saharan routes, and it was through Arab merchants that Islam began to make its impact. It was felt in Kanem earlier than anywhere else in Nigeria. Islam was probably making converts in Kanem as early as the eleventh century, at the end of which the ruler, *Mai* Hume (1085-1097), became a Muslim. The effect was greatly to increase the power and extent of the empire. The introduction of literacy and Arabic script, although confined to a tiny minority, created much greater administrative efficiency, extended commercial and diplomatic contacts further afield in North Africa, and did something to publicize the state abroad. Early in the twelfth century a *mai* made the pilgrimage to Mecca, and later in the century a pilgrims' rest house was built for Kanem-Bornu in Cairo. Arab and Muslim military ideas also played a part in expanding the state with the introduction of chainmail and elaborate cavalry accouterments after the twelfth century. But although Islamic influence undoubtedly increased the efficiency of the state, it seems to have had little effect on the ideology of power. There was no tendency to introduce Arabic feudal concepts, and the divine character and structure of the *mai*-ship persisted, despite the fact that it must have been clearly heretical. The power of the queen-mother persisted, despite the subordinate role assigned to women by Islam. It may therefore be concluded that Islam was a religion for the ruling classes in Kanem-Bornu, and was probably confined largely to the capital city, whereas the traditional divine kingship had to be maintained in order to secure the obedience of the rural agriculturalists who remained adherents of the traditional culture and religion.

In the two centuries after the introduction of Islam Kanem-Bornu extended its boundaries to become a formidable empire. Though expanding eastwards and westwards of Lake Chad, the greatest expansion was northwards, clearly in order to gain a larger share of the Saharan route to Tripoli. A wedge of territory extending up to and beyond Bilma, to the borders of Fezzan, was brought under control. Like other Sudanese states Kanem experienced serious difficulties of administering these conquered territories, where the loyalties inspired by divine kingship were flimsy; governors, often members of the royal kin, were despatched to rule the provinces. This had the effect of providing ambitious or unruly princes with a remote and secure base from which to arm their followers and hatch plots. In the early thirteenth century there were a number of such revolts, which were at first brought under control, only to erupt again at the end of the century when the Kanem empire almost collapsed in civil wars between members of the royal house. The empire became so weak that the Bulala people east of Lake Chad invaded the original center of the empire and expelled the ruling dynasty.

The state survived, however, for the dynasty moved southwestward of Lake Chad into Bornu proper, where they reformed the state. Their success was probably due to their ability to bring the trade route from Tripoli across with them by attracting the merchants to the new area. The move may also have had unforeseen economic advantages. The original Kanem area was in the northern part of the savannah, and the extent and elaborate nature of the empire indicate that it must have been based upon a more extensive agricultural base than the area would support today. It seems very likely that the area became overpopulated and overcropped, and destruction of the covering vegetation gave the Sahara its chance to advance further. An additional support for this view arises from the fact that the shift to Bornu seems to have been the shift of the whole Kanuri people, and not just of the ruling aristocracy. This is not a normal pattern of migration in Africa, and we must assume that the Kanuri agriculturalists were attracted by the better vegetation and rainfall conditions in Bornu. An original people, the So, were displaced so effectively that they have apparently left no surviving descendants. The Kanuri language thus spread southwards and eastwards inside the modern frontiers of Nigeria. The move appears to have taken some years to complete; the dynasty itself moved sometime in the 1380s, but the civil wars which had plagued them in Kanem seem to have continued for several decades. Toward the end of the fifteenth century the rebellions were effectively suppressed, the territory further expanded to the west, and some of the neighboring western states reduced to a tributary status and brought into close commercial relationship. Trade and diplomatic relations with Tripoli and the Fezzan were resumed, and some diplomatic correspondence in Arabic from Bornu still survives from this period. At the end of the fifteenth century, as if to symbolize the refoundation of the dynasty and the trade links across the Sahara, a new capital city was built by *Mai* Ali Gazi, named Ngazargamu.

Further west, during the centuries of the rise of Kanem and its transfer to Bornu, the unique civilization of Hausaland was developing at the same time. Its origins are obscure, and there seems little reason to presume that a non-Negro conquering group like the Zaghawa in Kanem-Bornu had any important role to play, despite the Hausa's own legends that their states were founded by six grandsons of an original immigrant who was a son of the King of Baghdad. The legend itself assumes an indigenous population, and the grandsons are the product of marriage to a Hausa queen, so that even the legend does not suggest foreign conquest. The influence of divine kingship also seems to have been much weaker in Hausaland, although it must be remembered that the original institutions may later have been much more modified by Islamic political ideology than in Kanem-Bornu. Some historians have suggested an important Berber element in the original creation of the states, but the diverse structure of the Hausa state system and the presence of many states hardly suggests a conquering aristocracy. The Hausa language is, however, distantly related to Kanuri, and thus to the Hamitic and Semitic tongues. It is probable that this is because the Hausa were originally a Saharan Negro people who colonized the savannah soon after A.D. 100 as a final southward shift prompted by Saharan desiccation and Berber pressures.

The Hausa civilization was characterized by a strong sense of cultural and linguistic identity without any political unity. There never existed anything which may be accurately termed a Hausa empire, and many of the states of Hausaland fell for long periods under foreign domination, yet their language and way of life not only persisted, but spread over West Africa until Hausa became almost a *lingua franca*. The basis for this cultural and linguistic unity and expansion was the highly developed commercial sense of the Hausa, who today can be found in every West African city as traders. The importance of trade in Hausa culture is revealed even by the legends related by the Hausa of their early history, in which the original states of the Hausa *Bokwoi* were said to have had specific duties and economic specialities: Gobir as the guardian of the northern frontier, Daura as the spiritual and religious center, Kano and Katsina as commercial centers, Zaria as the slave-trade center, and Rano as the industrial area.

The states of Hausaland were confined to the savannah area proper. Their economies were based on the channeling of the surplus agricultural production of the rural village peasantry into the towns, and each state was centered on a capital city. The city was a fortified bastion surrounded by huge mud walls, a permanent military base for the king's army, and the focus of the arts, crafts, and trades of the civilization. The economic basis of the civic culture was further augmented by slave trading and raiding of non-Hausa peoples to the south, by the great enterprise of individual Hausa merchants who moved south and southwestward in search of profitable forest products such as kola nuts, but above all by the strategic commercial positions of Kano and Katsina, the key cities of Hausaland, which lay at the southern end of the trans-Saharan caravan route from Tripoli. This route was the most important of all the routes across the desert, and apart from temporary disturbances due to wars or revolutions, was to remain so until the nineteenth century. Kano and Katsina were the marshaling centers for the products of Hausaland and the states with which it traded to the south. From here the Arab merchants bought slaves, gold, ostrich feathers, ivory, kola nuts, and leather in exchange for their imports of goods from Europe, North Africa, and the Near East: Venetian glassware, Arabic paper and parchments, cloth and beads, weapons and armor, salt, and silver.

Almost nothing is known of the early process of state-building in Hausaland. By the time of the earliest Arab writing on West Africa it is clear that the seven Hausa states were already flourishing communities, often at war with one another. In the fourteenth century Zaria, under the rule of Queen Amina, seems to have made a bid for supremacy, and to have placed several of the states as well as some non-Hausa areas to the south in a tributary position, but the supremacy of Zaria did not last.

The penetration of Islam into Hausaland has a significantly different history to that of Bornu. Despite the fact that the two cultures were neighbors, there is practically no evidence to suggest that early Islamic influences from Bornu entered Hausaland. Proselytization was much later and came from the west, when merchants from Mali began to spread the religion at the end of the fourteenth century. In Kano they persuaded the *sarki* (king) to build a mosque, observe ritual prayers, and appoint a priest and other Muslim officials. There is evidence that Islam was making ground in Katsina at the same time. Progress was slow, however; later rulers of Kano were pagans, and it is not until the fifteenth century that Islam gained a grip on the city life of Kano and Katsina. Islamic scholars from Timbuktu and North Africa now began visiting Kano and Katsina, teaching, preaching, and acting as political advisors to the kings. In the seventeenth century both towns began to produce scholars of their own, some of whose writings have survived. Islam had evidently taken firm root.

The development of Islam in Hausaland, however, invites comparison with Bornu. In Bornu Islam began its penetration five centuries earlier. Moreover, Bornu was a unified empire, whereas the political disunity of Hausaland produced a patchwork situation, in which Islam developed particularly in Kano and Katsina. In Zaria Islam seems to have made little impact until the nineteenth century, and in Gobir its impact was evidently slight. Even in Kano and Katsina Islam seems to have been a religion for the rulers and wealthy merchants. The kings were reluctant to adopt Islamic rules in political life and to abandon more traditional ways, for fear they would lose the traditional sanctions of authority over the masses of the people. Islamic practices were thus blended with traditional religious beliefs, for example in the way in which writing was used as a magical charm against evil spirits. Islamic purists naturally looked askance at such developments, and in the early nineteenth century this conflict was to provide the catalyst for revolutionary upheavals.

It was natural that Hausaland, politically disunited yet commercially wealthy, should prove an attraction to its neighbors, especially when its cities became centers of learning and therefore better known in the Muslim world. The first threat came from the west, where in the fifteenth century Sonni Ali built up the powerful empire of Songhai, centered on the city of Gao on the Niger. After 1504 Songhai armies moved into Borgu, taking the key Borguan towns of Ilo and Bussa on the Niger, which opened up navigation below the rapids at Bussa. In 1513 Songhai attacked Katsina itself, and in the next few years Kano, Zamfara, and Zaria were all attacked. The Hausa state of Kebbi now rose to become the focus of resistance, and in 1528 the Songhai armies were defeated, and much of Hausaland subjected to Kebbi overlordship. Bornu now intervened, but met with a series of defeats at the hands of Kebbi, which weakened Bornu until its revival in the reign of *Mai* Idris Alooma (1571-1603). Songhai again intervened seriously in Hausaland in the second half of the sixteenth century, but Songhai's empire collapsed in 1591 under the impact of a Moroccan invasion, in which firearms were used for the first time in the savannah area by the Moroccan troops.

The collapse of Songhai took place during a period of remarkable revival in Bornu, the work of *Mai* Idris Alooma. Idris was the earliest of the northern Nigerian rulers to perceive the advantages to be gained from external military aid; soon after ascending the throne he opened up close relations with Tripoli, from where he obtained Turkish musketeers to serve with his army. The Turks also began training Bornuan soldiers, and Idris imported large numbers of Arab horses across the Sahara to strengthen his cavalry. This new military strength was used first to subdue internal disaffection in Bornu itself, and then Kano was reduced to a tributary status. There was also considerable expansion eastward of Lake Chad at the expense of the now independent kingdom of Kanem. But the long term object of Idris Alooma's military policy was commercial: the early campaigns were preliminary to a series of important military advances northward, whose object was to secure the southern section of the caravan route across the Sahara. Campaigns against the Touareg of Air released the caravans from tolls and exactions levied by those Berber middlemen, while Idris finally occupied the key strategic oasis and salt-producing center of Bilma.

In civic government Idris determined to strengthen the influence of Islam. Early in his reign he made the pilgrimage to Mecca and organized the construction of a hostel for Bornuan pilgrims in the holy city. Great pressure was put on the Bornuan nobility to embrace Islam, and a chronicler of the time claims that all the most important aristocrats had become Muslim by the end of Idris' reign. Idris replaced many of the simple mud- or grass-built mosques with brick constructions, a new building technique which was quickly adopted to military and governmental building. But perhaps his most revolutionary innovation was the introduction of the *shari'a* (Muslim law) into the lower courts, which most closely affected the life of ordinary people. Here a conscious attempt was made to cut down the influence of customary African law, and to replace traditional chiefs and rulers by Muslim *qadi* (magistrates) either as actual judges or as legal advisors to the chiefs. Such developments were, of course, far from complete or universal throughout the empire, but they had the effect of further intensifying the impact of Islam in Bornu as compared to neighboring states, especially in Hausaland.

Both Bornu and the states of Hausaland were highly sophisticated urbanized polities, operating complex bureaucracies, which by this time were fully literate in Arabic script and much influenced by Islamic political ideas. It is important to stress, however, that even in the heartlands of these states Islam was still a religion of the governing classes, and especially of the urban inhabitants. Further south, in the area now known as the "middle belt," Islam had made no impact whatsoever. In this region a non-Islamic power made a significant, if ephemeral bid to control northern Nigeria: this was the Jukun state, based on Kororafa, a town which was situated south of the Benue. The meteoric rise and fall of the Jukun kingdom is still something of a mystery, for this illiterate people left no records of their own, and today they do not exist in Nigeria as a separate tribal group. What we know of them comes from Hausa and Bornuan references, which are naturally hostile. It is clear that they were organized as a typical African state of the divine-kingship pattern. The *aku* (king) was a divine and magical figure, surrounded by a paraphernalia of ceremonial and ritual designed to conceal his human nature from the people, and there are striking parallels with ancient Egyptian rituals.

The Jukun in the fourteenth century were tributary to Kano, and in the fifteenth century they were controlled by Zaria, but it appears that they established their independence in the sixteenth century, by the end of which they were becoming a threat to their neighbors. They had by this time organized cavalry troops, which operated rapidly over large distances in raiding parties (perhaps in imitation of the slave-raiding expeditions of Muslim cavalry who had in earlier times harried the Jukun). Zaria was forced to pay them tribute at the end of the sixteenth century, and in the seventeenth century the Jukun began to attack the centers of Hausa wealth and power. After 1650 they repeatedly attacked even Kano and Katsina in the far north, and in 1680 the Jukun invaded Bornu, where they were defeated. Though the Jukun continued to exist as a power, it would seem that from this time forward the Bornuans gradually reduced their strength, and may even have secured political over-lordship over the Jukun king. By the mid-eighteenth century the Jukun were no longer a force of significance in the power politics of northern Nigeria.

State-building in the Forest Area—Yoruba and Benin

We have seen that state-building in the savannah area of northern Nigeria arose from an original African basis of divine kingship whose rule and organization were originally made possible by agricultural advances and by iron tools and weapons, but which grew and expanded with the stimulus and opportunities made possible by contacts with the north across the Sahara. The importation of horses and camels, the wealth of the caravan trades, Arab and Berber military techniques, and the influence of Muslim political ideas and Arabic literacy all gave enormous advantages to the savannah zone. In the forest area, starting with the same agricultural revolution (though using different crops), iron technology, and divine kingship, Africans had to build their states without transport animals, without significant wealth from external trade in the formative centuries, and with no significant stimulus from contact with external cultures. When external contact came in the fifteenth century, it came not from Islam and North Africa, but from Christianity and Europe.

Of the history of the forest zone before A.D. 1,000 we know almost nothing except what may be suggested from linguistic evidence, i.e., that most of the indigenous stock of the Kwa subfamily of Negro

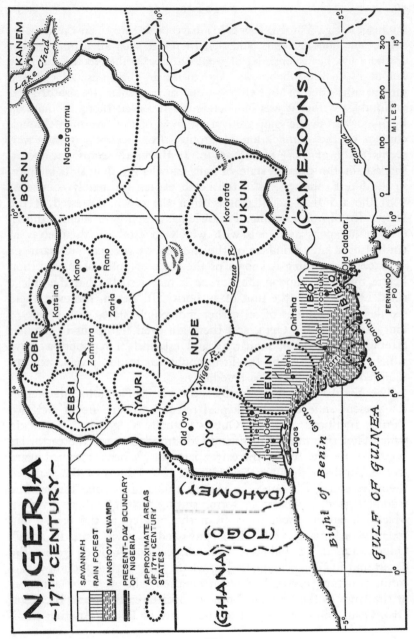

NIGERIA
~17TH CENTURY~

SAVANNAH
RAIN FOREST
MANGROVE SWAMP
PRESENT-DAY BOUNDARY OF NIGERIA
APPROXIMATE AREAS OF 17TH CENTURY STATES

KANEM

Lake Chad

BORNU

Ngazargarmu

GOBIR

Katsina

Kano

Rano

Zamfara

Zaria

KEBBI

YAURI

NUPE

Old Oyo

OYO

Ile-Ife

Ijebu-Ode

Lagos

(DAHOMEY)

(TOGO)

(GHANA)

Bight of Benin

GULF OF GUINEA

Gwato

BENIN

Benin

Warri

Brass

Bonny

Onitsha

Abor

Arochuku

BO

BI

Old Calabar

FERNANDO PO

(CAMEROONS)

Sanaga R.

Benue R.

Niger R.

Kororafa

JUKUN

MILES

0   100   200   300

55

languages (e.g., Yoruba, Ibo, Edo) have been spoken in the area for some four thousand years, and that therefore such alien immigration as there has been consisted of small groups unable to impose their languages on the inhabitants. Agriculture in the forest zone, based on the cultivation of root crops—yams in particular—is also of great antiquity, whether it was independently invented there, or built up by analogy from the grain-cultivating areas of the savannah through contact or the immigration of groups. Iron technology, however, seems to be of more recent origin. It therefore seems sensible to suggest, in the present state of our knowledge, that state-building in the forest zone was, as in the north earlier, intimately connected with the arrival of small groups from the north possessed of the knowledge of iron smelting, a knowledge which gave them a superiority of weapons and tools with which to establish themselves in control over large numbers of the indigenous villagers and farmers.

Practically nothing is known of the state of political organization before this time. Among the Yoruba it may well be that the village ruled by elders was the unit of authority. In Benin, however, there are definite traditions of an earlier indigenous state, with a line of kings known as the *Ogisi*, and there are even traditions of popular attempts to be rid of monarchy and establish a republic, a move which was frustrated by the first republican leader, Evian, who attempted to make his office hereditary.

The Yoruba traditions of origins are very difficult to interpret in the present state of archaeological research. There are in fact two Yoruba traditions of origin. One is virtually a "genesis" legend, in which God (Olorun) sent his son Oduduwa to create the earth. He began at Ile Ife, which thereafter has always been a sacred place to the Yoruba. Oduduwa then married the goddess of the sea, and their descendants became the various rulers of Yoruba towns. The second legend is secular in form, stating that Oduduwa lived in Mecca, where he broke away from the religion of the people and began worshipping idols. This provoked a civil war, in which Oduduwa and his followers were driven out, moving across the desert and finally reaching Ile Ife, where they settled. Oduduwa, according to this version, had seven children who were the ancestors of the kings of the six main Yoruba states in early times (Ila, Ketu, Oyo, Owu, Popo, Sabe) and of the rulers of Benin. Another tradition worthy of notice is that of a Yoruba relationship to "Gogobiri" (the Hausa state of Gobir) and Kukuwa (i.e., Bornu), whose original rulers, according to Yoruba legend, were brothers of Oduduwa. The tribal facial marks of the Yoruba are identical with tribal marks in these areas, so the legend appears to have some substance. In addition it must also be said that the Hausa traditions recognize "Yoruba" as one of the seven "illegitimate" or bastard states of Hausaland.

We may dismiss from the above legends not only the "genesis" aspects, but also the concept of origin from Mecca, which is clearly a late refinement designed to create a prestigious origin. The stories of a relationship to the north, however, contain no such motive, and are confirmed by Hausa ideas and by the tribal markings. It is therefore reasonable to suggest that the legendary first settlers were not "original" Yoruba—indeed they would not actually have been Yoruba speakers—but were in fact a minority group imposing their will on the indigenous people by the use of iron weapons which they brought with them. The idea of "offspring" of a single original founder is probably a simplification of a more complex process by which quarrels occurred among the ruling group and by which adventurers left to establish their own states, a process which may have taken a century or two to accomplish.

As with other African states, the new rulers would naturally try to legitimize their kingship by religious and magical sanctions. In this way Ife (a town which still exists as a Yoruba spiritual center, but which has probably shifted its site at least once, and perhaps several times) naturally assumed a special significance as a place of origin, and the new rulers of other Yoruba towns buttressed their control by claiming a special relationship with Ife, and seeking Ife sanction for their authority.

Most of the new states of what became known as the Yoruba empire were established in areas where the indigenous language was Yoruba. One state, however, was quite distinct, and this was Benin, itself destined to be a rival to Yoruba power. The Benin legend is that after the phase of the early indigenous kings and the failure of the republican movement, the people sent to Ile Ife to ask the king of that place to send a member of his family to rule over them. This legend may indeed be a euphemism to explain away the fact that a party from Ife conquered Benin, or it may indicate that the Bini people succumbed to the prestige of Ife's magical status. Whatever the explanation, Ife sent Prince Oranmiyan, according to legend a son of Oduduwa. The legend then goes on neatly to describe the process by which these immigrant rulers became "naturalized": Oranmiyan married a Bini princess and she bore him a son. After some years Oranmiyan renounced the throne in favor of this son, and is said to have made a speech in which he stated that "only a child, born, trained and educated in the arts and mysteries of the land could reign over the people." Thus a native dynasty began, but even so the connection with Ife was recognized, and at the death of every third *oba* (king) of Benin, his corpse was taken to Ife for burial.

Even for Benin, therefore, Ife remained a spiritual center. Ife itself developed in the twelfth and thirteenth centuries into a quite extraordinary center of civilization and artistic achievement. Unfortunately almost nothing is known of the economic and social background which made such a flowering possible, but such progress there must have been, together with a considerable political organization and marshaling of resources enabling specialization to take place and groups of craftsmen to emerge. As yet little is known about the normal civic life of ancient Ife, although even to see its archaeological sites—with their well-laid-out palaces and the beautifully constructed pavements of potsherds—is enough to indicate that this was a cultivated society, in which the rulers strove for comfort and sophistication. Ife is best known, however, for its sculpture in bronze and terra cotta. The terra cotta work was the earliest of Ife's artistic expressions, although work in this medium seems to have continued after the introduction of bronze. The terra cotta sculpture is particularly interesting in that its style is strikingly similar to that of the much earlier Nok culture, and this is one more link in the hypothesis of northern origins. The bronzes are triumphs of the human spirit. They were cast from the twelfth century onwards, by a most complex technical process known as "lost wax." Just how the Ife sculptors acquired this technique is a mystery; the same method was used by the ancient Greeks, but they could scarcely have transmitted it to Ife. An independent invention of the identical technique in Ife, however, seems too fantastic a coincidence to postulate.

Though technically extraordinary, the Ife bronzes are even more remarkable as works of art. Today they are treasured in museums the world over, and each one is virtually priceless. They are mostly presentations of heads, both male and female, which are naturalistic and representational, the features being expressed with fine beauty and delicacy. They are perhaps rivaled only by the stone sculpture of the ancient Greeks in the subtlety with which they portray the human face. The realism of these sculptures is also something of a mystery, for nowhere else in African art do we find this style; African art is normally abstract and much given to violent exaggerations of reality in order to achieve their particular effect (much as in the painting of such moderns as Matisse and Picasso, who were themselves close students of African art). Only in the art of Benin, where bronze casting was introduced from Ife in the fourteenth century, do we find this humanistic realism elsewhere in Africa. The explanation may lie in the purpose for which the sculptures were made, especially if their object was connected with a cult of ancestors whose likenesses the artist wished to immortalize.

The creation of such masterpieces in the Nigerian forest in the twelfth or thirteenth centuries was a fantastic achievement for a people who had but recently made the transition from stone to iron, a people without means of conveyance other than the canoe and the pan balanced on the human head, and with absolutely no contact or stimulation from even comparable, let alone more advanced, outside civilizations.

Despite its importance as a religious, cultural, and artistic center of Yoruba life, Ife never became a great center of power in southwestern Nigeria. It was not strategically located and was poorly placed to be of commercial importance, but above all it was inhibited politically by its position in the midst of the rain forest, and thereby by its lack of military mobility. Power in Yorubaland was to pass to the most junior foundation which sprang from Ife, the state of Oyo.

Oyo appears to have been founded to protect the Yoruba from Nupe and Borgu, states lying to the north between the Yoruba and the Hausa states. Oyo was thus situated in the savannah zone, and was well placed to act as a trading center for the dispatch of forest products northward to the Hausa, from whom the imports of the trans-Saharan trade could be obtained for re-export south to Ife and the other Yoruba towns. Oyo's beginnings were inauspicious, and the outpost was engaged in bitter struggle for survival with both Nupe and Borgu, often allying alternately with each. About 1550, when Nupe actually captured and conquered its territory, Oyo appeared to collapse, leaving the *alafin* (king) to flee in exile to Borgu. However, this defeat prompted the *alafin* radically to reform his army and to introduce cavalry as the main striking force. The *alafin's* new army surged back, the city of Oyo was rebuilt, and first Nupe and then Borgu were reduced to tributary status.

This was the prelude to the creation, in succeeding centuries, of a veritable empire which came near to unifying the Yoruba nation, and which was to survive until 1837. Besides pushing Oyo influences northwards (and thereby extending Oyo's trade) the armies of the *alafin* conquered the Yoruba states of Sabe and Ketu to the south, pushing down both sides of the Ogun River toward the sea, finally securing their outlet by securing commercial control of Porto Novo on the Atlantic coast.

Oyo was thus essentially a breakout by the forest-dwelling Yoruba into the savannah zone, where they exploited its military and commercial advantages, much as the Hausa had done at the terminals of the trans-Saharan caravan routes. Oyo now became the commercial center of the southwestern area of Nigeria, controlling contact with the north, charging tolls and profits on the trade, and, with its strong agricultural base, able to develop its own handicraft industries, of which the iron-smithing and cloth-weaving trades became famous.

The political organization of Oyo presents interesting comparisons and contrasts with the typical pattern of divine kingship. The *alafin* was never regarded as a god himself, though traces of the influence of divine kingship can be seen in his stress on the supposed divinity of his descent from Oduduwa, the son of God (although the variant tradition was that Oduduwa was a man from Mecca), but he was regarded as a companion of the gods, whom he was able to consult. The kingship was not despotic, but essentially constitutional and subject to rigorous checks and balances. The succession was never passed to the eldest son, for there was an excessive fear of patricide; instead, the eldest son was given the title *aremo*, and expected to commit suicide at the death of his father. The new *alafin* was chosen from among a limited number of royal candidates by the *oyo mesi*, a small number of privy councillors, amongst whom the *basorun* was pre-eminent, often serving as a kind of first minister. The Oyo constitution contained a complex system of proper action whereby legalized revolution could take place, for if the *oyo mesi* judged that the people, the gods, and the "earth" "rejected" the present *alafin* (usually because of unconstitutional actions on his part, or conspicuous failures) then the *basorun* solemnly presented the *alafin* with symbolic gifts—either a basket of parrots' eggs or an empty calabash—and it was the *alafin's* duty to commit suicide. There are several instances of this procedure being followed to the letter.

The administration of the expanding state, which by the seventeenth century was indeed a small empire in that it had begun to control non-Yoruba peoples, was neither feudal nor despotic. At the center, the *alafin* conducted an elaborate court ritual in his palace, assisted by numerous titled officials and eunuchs; in matters of state the *oyo mesi* led by the *basorun* were his principal advisors and assistants. In military affairs there was a separate bureaucracy, controlled by the *kakanfo* (commander-in-chief), who was also expected to commit suicide in the event of military defeat. Successful military commanders, however, could naturally act as a formidable check on the other parts of the constitution. A final additional check was the *ogboni*, a powerful and highly secret male society which had considerable functions, and needed to be consulted on vital matters of state, including any proposal to reject an *alafin* and force his suicide.

Local administration was of three kinds, that of Oyo territory proper, that of the subject Yoruba towns to the south, and that of non-Yoruba tributary areas. In Oyo territory proper each large town had its *oba* (king), each small one its chief, and the *oba* or chief was assisted by local councils composed of members of secret societies and lineage groups. In subject Yoruba areas the *obas* were supervised by *ilari* appointed from Oyo, who were in charge of tolls and taxes paid in kind. In the tributary areas there was no fixed Oyo officialdom; the tributary status was enforced by military power, and non-payment of tribute (often demanded in the form of slaves) was an open challenge to war.

The precise relationship between Oyo and Ife remains obscure. It seems quite likely that such was the spiritual and magical prestige of Ife that it remained independent of Oyo pressure, despite its relative weakness. Nor did Oyo become a cultural and artistic center to rival Ife. Oyo was more materialistic and power conscious, more concerned with trade and armies, while the non-Yoruba state of Benin, in fact, inherited more of Ife's cultural and artistic sense. In the middle of the fourteenth century the bronze casting technique was introduced from Ife, and Benin witnessed a similar flowering of the arts. Brass sculpture, of a style and beauty which has placed the medieval art of Benin second only to that of Ife, was used to record historical events, to immortalize *obas* and ancestors, or simply to provide things of decoration and beauty. The brass casting art also seems to have triggered off a flowering of sculpture and carving in other media—especially in wood and ivory—of an equally high artistic order. Besides the usual figures of men and animals, wood-carving was used on doors, doorposts, and furniture, to create gracious surroundings for the important houses of Benin city. In the four-teenth century, however, Benin was not yet a large empire or a rival to Oyo. Benin's rise to power awaited the opportunities presented by the coming of the Europeans after the fifteenth century.

The Ibo—A "Stateless Society"?

Thus, by the fifteenth century, northern and southwestern Nigeria already contained well-established states, each with several centuries of history and constitutional tradition behind it. In all these states the evidence indicates that the intrusion of minorities, usually coming from a northerly or northeasterly direction, and probably bringing iron-working techniques and iron weapons with them, was responsible for the formation of states with the patterns of divine kingship modified to suit local circumstances.

Along the lower Niger, however, and in the area east of that river, there is no evidence of either kingship, or even chieftaincy, before the late seventeenth century (when kingship institutions penetrated the Niger area from Benin). For the historian this raises acute problems of interpretation, made more difficult by the fact that the absence of kingship makes chronological problems more difficult, for lists of kings form a useful order of events, and events tend to be associated with particular kings in African traditions. The absence of kingship is even more puzzling in this area along and east of the Niger in view of the extraordinary cultural, linguistic, and social uniformity of the people who live there, the Ibo. The problem would be simpler if the Ibo were a stone age people: it could then be argued that the strength of their northern neighbors, and perhaps the rise of the Jukun empire in the sixteenth century, had shielded the Ibo from immigrant conquerors bringing iron weapons. However, the Ibo were as skilled in iron technology as any of their neighbors. The only hypothesis therefore, and it is no more than a hypothesis, is that the Ibo migrated into the area *en masse*, bringing their iron technology with them, and either completely expelled or destroyed the aboriginal inhabitants. To date such a movement is impossible, although it may be argued that Ibo dialects differ sufficiently for us to conclude that they must have been evolving in separate areas for perhaps a thousand years.

Whatever the explanation, the Ibo are distinct from the other major peoples in Nigeria in having evolved no centralized state or states, in the European sense of the term. Kingship and chieftaincy were unknown to them, even on the village level, until Benin influence made itself felt on the Niger in the seventeenth century. The Ibo culture nevertheless survived with remarkable uniformity, and the absence of a "state" in no way inhibited the economic or cultural achievements of the people. Ibo agriculture, indeed, was perhaps the most efficient in Africa, and Ibo population developed a density per acre only matched in Africa by that of the Nile valley. Though the Ibo village remained a sovereign law unto itself, the Ibo preserved a remarkable unity and conformity of customary law and practice, so that, even without a centralized state, they retained the social unity of a national group.

Each Ibo village was ruled by the council of elders, who were quite literally the old men. The old ruled because the basic assumption of Ibo political theory was that government was changeless and custom sovereign, and that the old must therefore be the most knowledgeable and experienced in custom. The function of the elders was entirely judicial, and their task was not only that of judging disputes, but also of suggesting decisions, in the light of their propriety according to custom. Innovations did occur, but only through the fiction that they were not truly new. The government of the elders was effected by the system of age-grades, in which the population was divided into sets of people of the same age with customary functions. Thus adolescent boys must keep the village streets clean and tidy, men in their prime were the warriors, and old men the councillors. Every matter did not engage the elders' attention, however, for the heads of families and the heads of "wards" of the village (an area or quarter supposedly composed of related families) dealt with disputes exclusively within their groups.

Such a system might seem at first sight to be a tyranny of conservatism, custom, and collectivism. This tendency was counteracted by the great play to individual enterprise and achievement given by various institutions, in particular the "title societies." These bodies were not truly political, for they had no functions of government except over their own members, but their leading figures naturally gained influence and prestige to affect decisions of the elders. They were, however, essentially bodies for the acquisition of status. They built up an elaborate hierarchy of titles, each superior to the one beneath it, which could sometimes be acquired by outstanding achievement (e.g., by deeds of valor in battle), but the general entry was obtained by wealth, measured in yams; titles could be bought by the payment of high entrance fees, together with the provision of elaborate feasts and presents for the existing members. The title societies thus became virtually a social security system, in which the wealthy farmer invested his "capital" from accumulated yam stores acquired in the prime of working life, gaining the return in "interest" in his old age, by reaping his share of fees and feasts from later new members. These societies became a built-in incentive to accumulate food supplies, even for those who failed to collect enough wealth to enter them. They played a vital role in the expansion of Ibo population. Later this drive for accumulation would be readily adaptable to the cash nexus, making the Ibo a driving force in Nigerian business and professional life during the colonial period.

Despite the absence of a "state," the Ibo also had common institutions and beliefs. The problem of relating these to Ibo historical development is still one which baffles historians. The village of Nri, near Onitsha, claims a status similar to that of Ife among the Yoruba, and there are Nri "genesis" legends of the village as a "garden of Eden" from which man emerged. It is interesting to note that the archaeologist Professor Thurston Shaw uncovered near Nri a remarkable series of bronze sculptures of great beauty, but in a style quite unlike that of Ife. Unfortunately it is still not possible to determine their date. The shrine of Aro-Chuku also had national significance for the Ibo, who believed that *Chuku* (God) dwelt in a cave in Aro, and spoke to the devotees who visited him much in the manner of the Delphic Oracle. In time Aro-Chuku became virtually a supreme court of Iboland, hearing appeals in important cases from the various localities, and levying fines. It will be seen that in later years the Aro-Chuku oracle exploited its position to become a vital cog in the slave-trade machine. Lesser oracles throughout Iboland served as regional tribunals.

State-building in Ghana

As already indicated, the evidence available to the historian in dealing with the history of Ghana before the coming of Europeans is scanty indeed; before A.D. 1,000 it is practically nonexistent except for stone age archaeological remains which have not been linked with any existing people in Ghana. What is certain is that the Akan peoples, the dominant group in modern Ghana, emigrated into Ghana in the two or three centuries after A.D. 1,000, and that the Akan migrations, with those of some non-Akan groups, set in motion the process of state-formation which was to create the pattern of states which dominated the history of the country until it fell under British rule in the later nineteenth century.

As is to be expected with so recent a conquest, considerable traces remain of the pre-Akan population, especially in the shape of the Guan-speaking peoples who still exist in numerous groups along the Volta River basin, and further north. It is also clear that the Guan language profoundly affected the speech of the Akan migrants, and the intermixture of Twi (the language classification of the Akan)

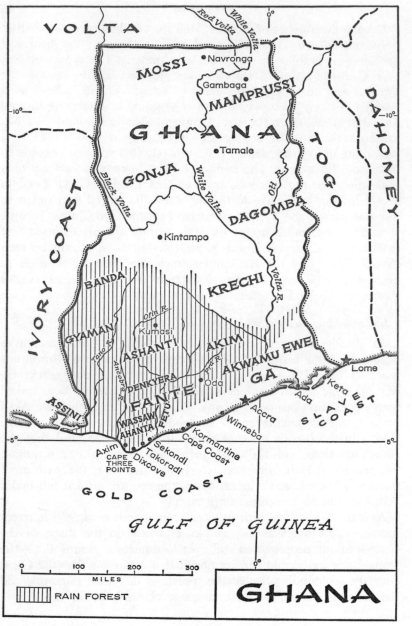

GHANA

and Guan in varying degrees produced various Akan dialects. Of the Guan political organization before the Akan conquest we know practically nothing.

The intrusion of the Akan, and the state-building which resulted in the forest and coastal savannah zone, was not of the same order as that which produced the Yoruba and Benin states in Nigeria, i.e., the establishment of foreign conquering minorities over local masses. The Akan evidently came in large groups, retaining their language. Generally it should seem that they pushed the Guan aside or, at the most, absorbed only minorities of Guan speakers, thus allowing the Twi language to be somewhat modified by Guan words. It is abundantly clear that the Akan brought with them a fully developed social and political system which they imposed virtually without modification, for even though the Akan fragmented into different "tribes" and formed a kaleidoscope of rival states, often at war with each other, the political theory behind these states and their detailed institutions remained practically identical Moreover, the clan organization of the Akan completely cut across these later state and "tribal" considerations. A Denkyera, for instance, would regard an Assin man belonging to his own clan as a "brother," would share identical taboos and totems with him, and would regard it as incestuous to marry a female Assin of his own clan. The clans therefore must be seen as preconquest institutions.

Many fanciful and fantastic ideas have been put forward about the original starting point of the Akan migrations—Mesopotamia, ancient Egypt, old Ghana, and North Africa have all been suggested. The Ghanaian historian Dr. A. Boahen more soberly concludes from Akan traditions that the Akan evolved in the area between the Black Volta and the Comoe Rivers on the western frontier of modern Ghana. The migrations themselves may have been touched off either by upheavals in the western Sudan, or by population pressure after A.D. 1,000. There were two groups of migrants, with separate routes, which may have moved at separate times. One group moved directly southward and settled to the west of the river Pra, where they later developed states such as Wassaw and Ahanta. The other moved southeastward, settling first perhaps as a single unit near the junction of the Pra and Ofin rivers, but later splitting, some moving farther southeastward to found the states of Akwamu and

Akim, others moving southward to found Fante and Aguafo, and still others swinging north. Akan groups probably reached the coastal areas and obtained access to the sea sometime between 1250 and 1350. By this time a basic state structure was in existence, but some of the most important African states in Ghana, including Ashanti, the most powerful of all, were later creations.

While the Akan were pushing in from the northwest, the Ga and Ewe were occupying the area of the Accra plain and the lower Volta. Though their languages are related, the Ga and Ewe are distinct groups who came into what is now Ghana in different ways. The Ewe simply pushed in from the southern Togo area, where several of them still live. The Ga, however, came from further afield in southern Nigeria, and although one group of Ga seems to have pushed overland, the other came by sea in large canoes. Their traditions tell of an original homeland near a "great river" and it may well be that they left Nigeria because of the upheavals which resulted from the establishment of Benin. The Ga established themselves around the mouth of the Volta, and continued to be a skilled canoe people. There is evidence to show that they remained in contact with Benin, carrying on a sea-borne commerce along the coast in the fourteenth century, and probably exporting gold which they obtained from inland Akan groups and importing cloth, beads, and perhaps slaves from the Benin area.

To what extent the geography of state-building in Ghana was influenced by commercial considerations is difficult to say. It is clear, however, that long-distance commerce had become common in the fourteenth century, and well-established patterns of trade were observed by the first Portuguese visitors in the fifteenth century. Besides the sea-borne east-west commerce controlled by the Ga, the Akan groups also traded with the remaining Guan groups, and with the Ga, for fish and salt. By about 1400 the Ga and Akan groups were beginning to build north-south routes to link up with the trade routes of the Sahara by making contact with the great commercial cities of the savannah, such as Timbuktu, Jenne, Kano, and Katsina. This trade was indirect, with the Akan merchants passing over their goods to northern middlemen at Tafo (where Hausa traders took them on to Hausaland) or going on to Begho, which had become a collecting point for goods which were taken on to Jenne or Timbuktu by merchants of Mali. The coastal area exported salt and cloth along this route, while the Akan states of the forest sent kola nuts to Hausaland, gold dust and slaves to Jenne and Timbuktu. In return they obtained beads and glassware (some of it Venetian ware brought from North Africa by the Arabs), weapons, and North African luxuries. As elsewhere, Islam also made its influence felt, especially north of the forest. Even among the Akan Muslims were treated with respect, gained positions as advisors in the state, and became influential. But in the forest area, or in the coastal plains, it never became a dominant influence on the scale which we have seen in northern Nigeria, for the forest area was too far from the really lucrative routes feeding the trans-Saharan trade to be of prime interest to the Muslims.

Thus, by the beginning of the fifteenth century, the Negro peoples of Ghana and Nigeria already had considerable achievements behind them. They had mastered the techniques of the agricultural revolution, applying them to both savannah and forest conditions, thereby enabling themselves to be fruitful and multiply, and to enjoy settled conditions in which surpluses could be accumulated for use in the support of handicraft industries, the arts, and religious observances. They had mastered the craft of working iron, and had colonized and peopled their countries. They had built states and systems of political and judicial authority. In the savannah these processes had been increasingly stimulated and developed after A.D. 1,000 by both Islam and literacy. Development in the forest had been virtually self-sustaining and without outside stimulus. The forest peoples, and especially the peoples of the immediate coast, were now to meet the formidable challenge of contact with Europe.

THREE

The European Impact

and the Slave Trade

The appearance of Portuguese ships on the west coast of Africa in the fifteenth century marked the beginning of a profound, if gradual, revolution in West African history. There had always been commercial contact with Europe, but it had been indirect, with North Africa acting as intermediary for European merchandise brought there by Genoese or Venetian merchants, who in turn took away the gold of the trans-Saharan trade to feed Europe's currency requirements. Such indirect contact meant that there was no European cultural or political impact. Trade, and political and cultural influence, ran along north-south lines, with the West African empires of the savannah zone reaping the benefit of their middleman position. The coming of Europeans was to lead to a gradual shift of the center of trade; the savannah zone was to lose its predominant position, and the Atlantic coast, instead of being on the edge of commercial life, was to become its center. The coastal states could now build for themselves a middleman position, which they could exploit for political as well as for commercial profit.

Portuguese motives in seeking to establish contact with West Africa were an inseparable blend of economic and religious considerations. Throughout the later middle ages the Christian states of the Iberian peninsula had been steadily expelling Muslim power from Spain and Portugal. At the same time more and more rumors of the trans-Saharan gold trade filtered through, despite Arab attempts to keep it secret. In 1415 the Portuguese crossed the Straits of Gibraltar and took the North African fortress of Ceuta from the Muslims. Among the conquerors was Prince Henry the Navigator, who immediately began collecting information about West Africa from Arab and African traders in the area. He was particularly con-

71

cerned with the prospects for a gold trade, and with the possibility of discovering Christian kingdoms in West Africa, with whom he could form alliances and plan concerted attacks on the Muslims in north Africa. (This conception was, in fact, based on the rumors received in Europe about Ethiopia, the Christian empire in Northeast Africa.) The idea was thus generated of turning the flank of the Muslims by a direct approach along the as yet unexplored West African coast.

Portuguese ships began moving down the coast after 1420, but initially these voyages were little more than piratical raids against the Barbary Coast. After 1433 the ships began pushing boldly south in search of non-Muslim peoples, and by the 1450s they had established contacts with the Negro peoples of the Gambia-Senegal area. Here they began penetrating inland up the rivers, searching for the sources of gold and attempting to found interior posts which could straddle the trans-Saharan trade routes and divert commerce to the coast, but without success.

In the 1460s a decisive step forward brought the Portuguese into contact with what is now Ghana; Fernao Gomes, a merchant of Lisbon, was granted a monopoly of trade beyond Sierra Leone, on condition that his ships explore a further one hundred leagues of coastline each year. Gomes' ships eventually lighted upon the coastline of modern Ghana, where the Portuguese began to obtain gold at last. The trade was so lucrative that King John II resumed Gomes' monopoly and began direct exploitation of the trade. In 1482 the Portuguese built the castle of Sao Jorge da Mina in the center of what they were now calling the *Costa da Mina* (coast of the mine), and which the English would later call the Gold Coast. In 1502 they built a subsidiary fort at Axim, and in the last years of the fifteenth century about 3,000 pounds of gold flowed into Lisbon each year. Further east the Portuguese made contact with the kingdom of Benin. Here it seems that the *oba* permitted no fortifications, although a trading post was maintained from about 1485 until about 1505. In Benin there was no gold, but the Portuguese did a lucrative trade in pepper, and for the first time began a small slave trade. The early voyages in the first half of the fifteenth century had indulged in a good deal of slave raiding, but the Portuguese had not developed a slave export from the Gold Coast; indeed, the Gold Coast was an area in which slaves were in demand, for very little labor was needed to carry the precious small parcels of gold to the sea coast, whereas large numbers of men were needed to carry the Portuguese imports of European goods into the interior in exchange. The Portuguese thus began buying slaves from Benin for sale on the Gold Coast.

The gold trade, however, remained in the forefront of Portuguese activity, with the slave trade a subsidiary, if growing, commerce. The slave trade was dependent upon the growth of plantation economies, and began with the colonization of the off-shore islands by Portuguese settlers. Sao Tome was developed in this way early in the fifteenth century, and by 1520 was the center of an organized slave trade from Benin. Slaves were absorbed into the island's economy; some were sent to Lisbon where they were later sold to the new Spanish island colonies in the West Indies, and some were exported to the Gold Coast. In 1530 the Portuguese began shipping slaves directly to the Spanish West Indies, but even at this late stage the total trade from Sao Tome was little more than a thousand slaves a year.

Before 1530, in fact, it must have seemed that contact with Europe was to be wholly beneficial for the coastal regions. From the island settlements such as Sao Tome, surrounding African peoples obtained and diffused a host of new plants which greatly diversified the West African agricultural economy, improved the quality of the African diet, and introduced new staples which allowed the population to rise steadily in the subsequent centuries. Citrus fruits and melons were introduced from southern Europe, and when the Portuguese moved around into the Indian Ocean after 1498 they brought back the coconut and Asian yam to West Africa. But the greatest indirect service performed by the Portuguese for West African agriculture was the introduction, very rapidly after Columbus' discovery of the new world, of a whole complex of American crops, including maize, pineapple, pawpaw, sweet potatoes, guavas, and tomatoes. Maize was the most important of these in its effect upon population growth, because it provided an additional staple to yams. Cassava, another American Indian plant, was to prove equally important, but it was not introduced into West Africa until much later. It is ironical that the introduction of these new crops, making possible extensive population growth, should have taken place only a few decades before Europe began systematically to transport millions of West Africans to America as slaves.

The first years of Portuguese impact also seemed likely to benefit West Africa in the cultural sphere. Christianity, by spreading the skill of literacy in the Roman script, could have done for the coastal region as much as Islam with its Arabic script and political ideas had done for the savannah states in late medieval times. The Portuguese were indeed full of proselytizing zeal, and took care to deal with "pagan" rulers with delicate care. Africans from Benin and the Gold Coast were taken to Portugal and treated as "brothers" by the court nobility; some were educated to a high standard for the priesthood. High hopes were entertained for the conversion of rulers such as the *oba* of Benin, in the belief that they would convert their masses to Christianity. The *oba* did, indeed, order one of his sons and some of the chiefs to become Christians, a church was built in Benin, and Portuguese missionaries were received. Many Binis, including the *oba* and his court, learned Portuguese which, by the mid-sixteenth century was becoming a *lingua franca* of trade along the coasts. In the kingdom of Warri, south of Benin, missions had their greatest success, and the religion survived for nearly two centuries. On the Gold Coast the Portuguese cultural impact was even stronger, because of their permanent presence in the forts, where Catholic chaplains served the white traders and made converts among Africans.

Nevertheless, the cultural impact was slight. The missionaries were overly sanguine in believing that if they could convert rulers the people would follow. They failed to realize what African rulers were only too well aware of—that the traditional religion and the divine aspects of kingship were a powerful political force which African rulers had no reason to abandon. More progress might have been made if the Portuguese had concentrated more on the educational aspects of Christianity. Africans were eager to learn, and quickly realized the usefulness of literacy both for commerce and government. However, the bulk of Portuguese visitors were themselves illiterate, unlike the Arab traders of the savannah, and the literate Portuguese governors and merchants had neither time nor inclination for teaching. Even the missionaries regarded oral catechism preparatory to baptism as more important than literacy. The Catholic faith was not a Bible-reading religion.

Finally, what slow progress the Portuguese had made was interrupted first by their Asian colonization, and then by Protestant rivals. Once the Portuguese had made contact with India and the East Indian islands in the early sixteenth century, the profits obtainable in Asia led to the neglect of West African opportunities. The Benin pepper trade was abandoned, and trade establishments in Benin withdrawn. The missionaries died of disease and were not replaced. The slave trade continued, but it was organized from Sao Tome. Exactly at the time the Portuguese were lessening their hold on West Africa, competition from other European traders began. After 1530 it appeared that the French would be Portugal's chief rivals, but in the second half of the sixteenth century the wars of religion in France gave the Dutch and English their opportunity, and it was the Dutch who first seized the predominant position.

Dutch intervention was at first gradual; their ships began frequenting the coast at the end of the sixteenth century, and in 1596 they actually attacked the great Portuguese fort at Sao Jorge da Mina, but failed to take it. In 1612 the Dutch constructed their first fort, under the protection of the Gold Coast king of Saboe, at Mouree close to the Portuguese. Because they were more efficient traders, and carried cheaper goods, they were often welcomed by African rulers, who wished to see competition between European suppliers. By the early seventeenth century the Dutch had become the predominant European traders on the coast, often making as many as thirty voyages a year to the Gold Coast. In 1621 they formed the Dutch West India Company as part of a grand design. The company was given a monopoly of trade with the Americas and with West Africa, and its object was no less than the destruction of the Portuguese empire in the Atlantic. In 1630 the Dutch began the attempt to seize Brazil from Portugal; in the next ten years the Dutch settlements on the West Indian islands were established, and in 1637 a fleet was assembled in Brazil to attack Sao Jorge da Mina and drive the Portuguese from the Gold Coast. The strategic plan was ominous for the future of West Africa, for it clearly showed that the Dutch were aware of the need to secure a permanent slave supply if they were to develop their West Indian islands and their new colony of Brazil. The fleet of 1637 was victorious, and the Portuguese expelled; Sao Jorge was now renamed Elmina, and became the center of Dutch power in West Africa. By 1642, with the capture of Axim, the Dutch had expelled the Portuguese entirely from the Gold Coast. The Dutch failed, however, to expel the Portuguese from Sao Tome island, and thus Portuguese slave trading in southern Nigeria continued.

The Dutch also failed to secure Brazil, from which they were expelled by the Portuguese in 1654. This did not, however, mean that Dutch dreams of an Atlantic empire in the West Indies, based on the development of tropical plantation agriculture with African slave labor, came to an end. With a few West Indian islands of their own, the Dutch now became the carriers for the French, English, and Spanish colonies in America. From 1630 onward the West Indian islands witnessed the sugar revolution, in which earlier activities— such as ranching, logging, and mining, which had been performed by white and Indian labor with only a sprinkling of Negro slaves— were almost entirely displaced by sugar cultivation. The sugar revolution was an unmitigated disaster for West Africa, for it created an insatiable demand for African slave labor. Not only did this demand push up the numbers enslaved into tens of thousands each year, but it also created highly competitive conditions in which, during the seventeenth century, practically every country on the Western seaboard of Europe, including Sweden, Denmark, France, Holland, England, Portugal, and even Brandenburg, entered into competition for the trade. A single monopoly would at least have been a more controlled and restricted affair. From 1650 the competing European nations began selling firearms and ammunition in return for slaves on a large scale. Once begun, this could not be stopped by any nation which wanted to remain in the trade.

The English first began serious attempts to develop their own slave trade under Cromwell, when the sugar revolution in the English West Indies had already begun to demonstrate the dangers of reliance on the Dutch for the slave supply. Further attempts to organize chartered companies after the Restoration of the Stuarts in 1660 were indifferently successful, until in 1672 the Royal African Company was formed. The new importance of the slave trade in the

English imperial system was highlighted by the important part played by the royal family in its shareholding, with the king's brother, James, Duke of York (later James II), as its leading figure. The company was to last in this form until 1750, and under its organization the English slave trade fought its way against Dutch rivalry to the predominant position in the eighteenth century. Like other nations, the English found that the monopoly could not be enforced, and the lion's share of the trade fell to "interlopers" from Bristol and Liverpool, who built those ports into great cities on the profits of the African, West Indian, and American trades. After 1750 the Royal African Company was replaced by the Company of African Merchants, which had no monopoly, but which was allowed to charge customs duties to pay for the administration of English forts in the Gold Coast and elsewhere along the coast.

The Effects of the Slave Trade

The eclipse of the Portuguese and the rise of Dutch and English influence brought to an end any possibility of a cultural flowering of coastal Africa stimulated by European Christianity and literacy. The Dutch and English showed no interest in missionary activity and, of the handful of Africans who came to Europe and received higher education, scarcely one returned home to lands where there was nothing profitable for them to do except slave trading. Although some Africans around the forts in the Gold Coast became literate, they usually used their skill as clerks for slave traders.

Not only did the slave trade kill possible stimulus from contact with Europe, but it also may have seriously retarded progress which Africans were already making before the 1640s. Looked at from almost any point of view, the slave trade militated against economic and social development. It provided an easy living for ambitious and sufficiently ruthless Africans, who might otherwise have had their enterprise forced along more socially useful channels. It channelled off surplus population which might otherwise have created social problems requiring economic advances for their solution, and it took away precisely those fit men and women in their prime who would have contributed most to society. To supply the European traders with their slaves, African middlemen had to raid their interior neighbors, a process which became even more destructive with the introduction of firearms. In areas subject to slave raiding, and its consequent looting and destruction of crops, any incentive to accumulate stores and treasure (the African equivalent of capital accumulation without which no economic advance was possible) was destroyed. Moreover, European imports of textiles, metals, basins, weapons, beads, and the like—so easily obtainable for slaves—led to a serious decay in African industries, so that many techniques, especially in metal working, disappeared completely. Though the slave trade, as will be seen, did build up certain powerful states which were bound to produce some cultural by-products, in general it may be said that the slave trade, being itself a coarse, brutal, and degenerate human activity, produced in African cultures a general coarsening and brutalizing effect. No African society in the slave trade period produced art of a delicacy and subtlety comparable to the Ife bronzes, and the degeneration to crudity and coarseness of style in Benin art steadily increased after the seventeenth century.

The fantastic and ever-increasing scale of human suffering over two centuries and more, though incapable of historical analysis, was, however, the worst aspect of all. For every African transported against his will to America, another certainly died in the internal fighting necessary to sustain the trade. In a society entirely constructed of family relationships, the anguish of transportation can scarcely be imagined, and life as a slave across the water offered in compensation only a life of constant manual drudgery with the whip as the only incentive. As a crime against humanity the slave trade had no rival until the camps of Nazi Germany.

An additional refinement of degradation was the willingness of Africans, given the European demand for slaves, to provide the supply. Except for the early days of the trade, and for isolated "interlopers" in the trade, Europeans themselves did not catch their slaves or directly engage in warfare or raiding for them. Indeed, had they attempted to do so it is certain that African coastal rulers would not have permitted it. Even the European forts on the Gold Coast were not "colonies"; the ground upon which they stood was recognized as falling under African sovereignty, and regular "rent" was usually paid to African rulers. The coastal kings were determined to reap their share of the profits of the trade, and Europeans were not permitted to penetrate inland where they might procure their own slave supply. Whether resident in "factories" or forts, as in the Gold Coast, or simply lying off shore in their ships as they did in southern Nigeria, the Europeans on the coast were definitely in a subordinate position vis à vis African authorities; they always paid taxes on the trade, were made to open trade with elaborate presents to the king and his influential subjects, and in some places even had to take out formal licences to trade. It is ironical to note that, while the growth of slavery in the Americas was a root cause of the growth of ideas of Negro racial inferiority, the trade in West Africa bred an elaborate and formal system of "equality" in relations between the European traders and their African middlemen. The Europeans were in no position to risk giving insults, and took pains to wine and dine their African hosts and to mix with them on terms of joviality.

The institution of slavery had been a formal part of most, though not all, West African societies before the Atlantic trade developed. Slavery often originated as the lot of groups conquered by a more powerful invading force, and thus hereditary slave castes developed in some societies. A man could also fall into a state of slavery through irredeemable debts. In the Gold Coast such men became "pawns" until the debt was paid, perhaps by a relative or friend. In Ibo country people reduced to abject poverty could throw themselves at the mercy of a religious shrine, but by so doing they and their descendants became "osu" and perpetual outcasts of society. In most societies some serious crimes also carried the penalty of enslavement.

Such institutions were easily adapted to supply the demands of slave traders. In the savannah zone there had been an export of Negroes to North Africa and the Middle East since ancient times, and the influence of Islam, with its doctrine that it is the duty of believers to make war against the pagan and enslave those who refused the True Faith, intensified this process. In the south the European demand was first met by intensifying the enslavement of criminals and debtors, but it was inevitable that the process should be soon extended, especially with the introduction of firearms after 1650, by seeking the major source of supply in the form of war captives.

The African States in the Era of the Slave Trade

Once the slave trade began to develop and expand after 1650, it became a commerce of a magnitude which eclipsed previous trading contacts with Europe, and apart from agriculture was the chief economic activity of African states who had direct coastal contact with Europeans. With the introduction of firearms it took on a political aspect which African rulers could ignore only at the peril of their continuing power. Leaving morality aside, for the states of the coast and forest area the choice was between slave trading and acquiring "modern" weapons, or abstention from the trade and falling prey to rivals. Power politics in the south of Ghana and Nigeria thus took on a desperate aspect of the survival and dominance of the fittest. This factor was profoundly to affect the state-building process, already well under way in pre-European times. In both Nigeria and Ghana the process was basically similar—the struggle between coastal and interior states for control of access to Europeans and the acquisition of firearms.

In Nigeria Benin was the first to be affected by European contact. The Portuguese arrived about 1485 and began the trade in pepper for Europe and slaves for the Gold Coast. Their fruitless missionary efforts and withdrawal of permanent representatives after about 1505 have already been mentioned. Nevertheless, Benin continued to be a center of commercial activity, building up a considerable seaport at Gwato, where the Portuguese continued to buy slaves for transportment to Sao Tome. English ships made their appearance in the sixteenth century, and by the seventeenth century French, Dutch, Portuguese, and English were all trafficking in Benin. Benin policies reacted accordingly. There had been little European contact with the area between the forts of the Gold Coast and the Benin coast until this time, and Benin armies in the seventeenth century fanned out eastward and westward to secure control of as much of the coastline as possible. Westward they cut off the short southward route to the sea for Oyo and the Yorubas by reducing the coast as far as Lagos to Benin control. Eastward they pushed through the delta of the Niger and across as far as Bonny. This expansion was intended to monopolize the trade of the interior, and at the same time the wars themselves provided slaves for sale to the

Europeans. In the seventeenth century the policy seemed completely successful.

Such wide-spread expansion meant that it was not possible to control the subjected areas closely in day-to-day administration, and local rulers, often of Benin origin, were given considerable autonomy within a structure of suzerainty from Benin, although, on the death of a local chief, the successor would need confirmation from Benin, and might even have to visit Benin to be installed.

Benin influence also expanded inland and northward up the great Niger River during the seventeenth century, probably a result of Benin activity in the delta areas and the desire to tap the vast slave resources of the Ibo population of the interior. The use of armed canoes, huge vessels fitted with imported European cannon, provided a means of intensifying the exploitation of the Ibo. Whether the intrusion of small groups of Benin conquerors up the Niger was directly controlled by the *oba* and his government is doubtful; it seems more likely that the intruders were his disaffected nobles or relatives looking to carve a fortune for themselves from the sources of slave supply. At Aboh and Onitsha they established themselves as rulers, introducing the monarchical system (patterned on the obaship at Benin) among the Ibo, who had hitherto governed themselves without chieftaincy. Benin influence even extended as far into the interior as Idah, now in the Northern Region of Nigeria. A vast and complex network was established in which the Ibo of the interior were subjected to periodic raiding, often from hilltop fortresses garrisoned by the raiders, and the captives transported overland to the nearest river station, there to be packed in canoes and sold and resold, passing through the hands of many middlemen before reaching the European ships.

At first it must have seemed that the results of the trade were to mean indefinitely extended control and conquest for the African state which, like Benin, could be first in the field. Slaves brought profit which could buy more arms and feed more soldiers for even wider conquests. For Benin, however, the trade also brought ultimate ruin. The logic of the trade was force and greed for profit, and those on the peripheries of the empire, especially if they were situated on the coast and able to make contact themselves with Europeans, were tempted to bid for independence, to repudiate tolls and tributes to

Benin city, and to attempt to engross all the profit for themselves. Such feelings were even stronger where the people were not themselves Binis. Throughout the eighteenth century Benin suffered this fate as the outlying provinces fell away and the slave supply was obtained from nearer and nearer home by civil wars and attempts to crush the rebels.

One of the first areas to fall away from Benin control was the Niger delta itself, and here there developed a chain of remarkable city-states, built on slave trade foundations, which were to become the center of the trans-Atlantic trade in the eighteenth century. The peoples of this coast were of three distinct groups: to the west of the Niger and south of Benin there emerged the Itsekiri state of Warri; in the central and eastern delta area the people who built the city-states of Brass (or Nembe), New Calabar (or Kalabari), and Bonny were Ijo; further east and outside the delta of the Niger proper, the Efiks created the city-state of Old Calabar (now simply called Calabar).

The remarkable thing about all these states is the way in which they were built up as powerful and prosperous communities in response to the stimulus of the commercial opportunities offered by the trade. The land on which they were built was unable to support life by agriculture, being predominantly mangrove swamp. The city-states originated as fishing and salt-panning villages, eking out a precarious living by exchanging these commodities with the Ibo agriculturalists of the forest areas behind them. With the arrival of European slave ships the delta peoples seized their opportunity. A canoe people from their origins, they now began constructing monster vessels and arming them with brass cannon bought from Europe. With these they carved out "spheres of influence" in the interior, euphemistically termed "markets." Short of manpower and population, they retained thousands of Ibo slaves for themselves, incorporating them into the canoe teams as "puller boys" for the further prosecution of the trade. Because they were not plantation slaves, and could not therefore be disciplined in closely controlled gangs, the city-state freemen created a special and peculiar type of slave status for the Ibo. The slave became a member of the "house," an institution which was really a vast extension of the traditional African family which now incorporated the canoe teams under an elected house head (referred to as the "father"). Slaves of ability and intelligence were loaned trade goods and allowed a percentage of profits, and such personal property was allowed them by law. Slaves could accumulate enough property to buy their freedom and could even become heads of houses. The "career open to talents" thus prevented any possibility of slave rebellion under the most intelligent leaders, for wealthy slaves themselves became slave owners and were often fanatical defenders of the system.

There thus arose an extraordinarily complex social system in which there were two sets of social values. Freemen still maintained an attitude of superiority to the slave and ex-slave classes, paying respect to the "nobles" and high born members of the royal family above them, glorying in their own name of "freeborn," and contemptuously referring to those beneath them as "niggers" (a term having no color connotation whatsoever). But these gradations bore increasingly little relationship to class based on wealth, and by the eighteenth century freemen of little wealth might be engaged in manual labor while some slaves were occupied entirely in trade organization. A quite different classification thus emerged side by side with gradations of birth, in which a wealthy slave was termed a "gentlemen," and any manual worker was termed a "boy." In one respect, however, birth counted for all, for it was universally recognized, even by the wealthy slaves, that no slave could ever assume the sacred office of kingship.

Perhaps nowhere in Africa did economic considerations so profoundly affect the shape of society as in the Niger delta. Though the original cultural identities of the Itsekiri of Warri, the Ijo of Brass, New Calabar, and Bonny, and the Efik of Calabar maintained different overall systems of government (monarchies among the Itsekiri and Ijo, a republican form in Calabar), the house system, as the unit of trade, permeated all of them. Moreover, the absorption of large numbers of Ibo east of the Niger produced an extraordinary cosmopolitan effect, in which most cities became trilingual, speaking the native Ijo or Efik, Ibo, and pidgin English, the language of trade with Europeans. By the end of the eighteenth century there were even rudimentary schools in Calabar for the teaching of pidgin English, reading and writing, with the object of producing clerks and bookkeepers.

No one city-state ever succeeded in unifying the coast under a single government. During the eighteenth century there were a series of wars, especially between New Calabar and Bonny, which essentially took the form of struggles for interior markets. By the end of the eighteenth century each city-state controlled well defined areas of hinterland territory. The cultural life of the city-states was brash, materialistic, and sophisticated, reflecting its commercial basis. The kings and heads of houses lived well and luxuriously, importing all manner of goods from Europe, including liquor in large quantities, pictures, mirrors, silver cutlery, china and glassware, silks, fine clothes, and—at the end of the eighteenth century—elaborate prefabricated houses constructed by shipbuilding firms in Britain. They also imported huge quantities of gunpowder, muskets, and cannon.

It is probable that the city-states simply raided their "markets" in the hinterland at first, but by the eighteenth century the trade had become much more organized and, in a peculiar sense, "peaceful." This development was very much the work of the Aro people, living some forty miles behind the coast. Aro was the site of the great oracle of Aro-Chuku, a huge cave where Chuku, the Supreme Being, was supposed to have dwelt. The oracle was revered and respected by all the Ibo hinterland, by the Efik, by the Ibibio in their rear, and by the Ijo, and acted as a supreme court for all these peoples, deciding cases too important or too difficult for local justice. With the development of the slave trade the Aro people began systematically exploiting their oracle for profit. Groups of Aro began moving east and northeast to found settlements across the north-south trade routes in the Ibo interior. Here they settled not as conquerors, but virtually as legal "touts," systematically fomenting disputes and encouraging the litigants to take their cases to the Aro-Chuku oracle. Once at Aro the litigants, always important men accompanied often by hundreds of followers, were subjected to systematic economic exploitation. They were not allowed into the town itself, but forced to await "the law's delay" in the forest near the cave of Chuku, where the Aro sold them food at exorbitant prices often for months on end. When the case was heard a gigantic fraud was perpetrated; the belief was that after each party had stated its case before the mouth of the cave, God (Chuku) would personally speak his verdict from within, and the losing party must then enter the cave to be literally eaten by God. In fact, a priest spoke from within, and when the unfortunate losers entered, they were quickly clubbed and bound by waiting strong-arm men, packed in canoes behind the cave, and shipped down river as slaves.

The Aro oracle dominated the slave trade of the area behind Calabar, but it was not the only source of supply. The lack of central authority among the Ibo and the resultant perpetual inter-village disputes constantly fed the trade, and the network of creeks and rivers provided a transport system extending far into the interior. On the Niger the towns of Idah, Onitsha, and Aboh each in turn acted as middlemen, until Aboh transported the slaves to merchants from Brass or New Calabar.

Unlike Benin, the city-states of the delta did not eventually collapse under the impact of the trade which made them rich. In this respect they were unique, and the explanation lies in their extraordinary adaptability and willingness to come to terms with new conditions. Even when the slave trade was finally abolished, it did not mean the end of the city-states; they rapidly adapted their commercial supremacy to the new conditions of the nineteenth century.

It has been seen that almost all the Nigerian coastline in the slave trade period had fallen under the control either of Benin (from Lagos to the Niger delta) or of the city-states (from the delta to Calabar). This left the Yoruba empire of Oyo hemmed in and prevented from contact with the Europeans by the short north-south route. Moreover, the formative centuries of Oyo's rise had not fitted her for participation in the trade—her center of gravity was the edge of the savannah, where the formidable Oyo cavalry could operate, and her commercial ambitions looked northward to the Hausa trade and through them to the Sahara. The early Oyo wars and expansion had been northward into Borgu and Nupe. With the advent of the slave trade Oyo began to reconsider the direction of her expansion. Benin must have been regarded as too formidable a foe, and there seems to have been no attempt by Oyo to wrest control of Lagos, which would have been the natural outlet to the sea. Instead Oyo looked farther westward, skirting the area of Benin suzerainty, and attempted to dominate the towns of what is now the eastern coastline of the Republic of Dahomey, and in particular the seaport of

Porto Novo. By the end of the seventeenth century Oyo had reduced Porto Novo to tributary status, and crushed attempts at independence by a series of punitive expeditions.

The route from Oyo territory to Porto Novo, however, was long, circuitous, and difficult, and in the early eighteenth century Oyo was challenged by the rise of Dahomey, which lay north of Porto Novo and wished to obtain its own outlet to the sea. In 1724 the Dahomeyans swept south, and relieving forces from Oyo were defeated. In 1727 Dahomey again invaded, this time seeking to impose control on Whydah, another seaport west of Porto Novo. Oyo forces now struck at Dahomey proper, and in 1729 the king of Dahomey sued for peace, promising to pay tribute to Oyo. But this was not the end of the struggle; the tribute was not paid, and Oyo again invaded Dahomey in the 1730s. Finally Dahomey capitulated and paid tribute after 1747. Oyo's outlet to the sea was apparently secure.

The long wars and the rising extent of the slave trade began to produce decay and decadence in Oyo similar to that seen in Benin. In Oyo this manifested itself in a serious lessening of respect for kingship, and a rising cult of ruthlessness and violence in the capital, symbolized by the career of Gaha, the *basorun*. The office of *basorun*, as has been seen, was essentially that of the king's chief advisor, and it also carried the power of deposing the *alafin*, provided the proper constitutional forms were observed. Gaha ruthlessly perverted these traditions to serve his personal power. Immediately on his appointment Gaha murdered the chief supporters of *Alafin* Labisi, and forced the *alafin*'s suicide. The next *alafin* ruled only 130 days before he was murdered by Gaha. Two succeeding kings, one of whom at least succeeded in poisoning Gaha so that his legs became paralyzed, were also forced to suicide for their unamenable ways. Finally *Alafin* Abiodun, around 1780, organized a popular uprising which placed him in effective control; Gaha was captured and burned to death on the wood of his own palace.

There followed, during the remaining years of the reign of Abiodun, a kind of Indian summer of the Oyo empire. The brutalities and terrorism of Gaha's dictatorship, unsanctified by tradition, were ended, and internal peace and harmony seemed to return. However, there were already signs of ominous cracks in the imperial structure; in the early 1780s Dahomey repudiated her tributary status, and Oyo armies failed to punish the defiance. Oyo's trade routes to the sea thus became dangerously insecure. The northern tributary areas began to break away and secure protection from the Hausa. But worst of all, the heartland of the Yoruba territories began to crumble when the Egba group declared their independence and defeated Abiodun's punitive expedition. The Egba lay across the approaches to the south and the sea. Thus began a process by which each section of the Oyo empire and the Yoruba nation was to seek its own immediate advantage, and in which the Yoruba nation was to collapse under internal disunity and external threat in the early nineteenth century.

On the Gold Coast the coming of Europeans had effects on the African political map equally as profound as those we have seen in Nigeria, and here again it is in the period after 1650, when the slave trade with its attendant imports of firearms displaced the earlier trade in African products, that the biggest changes occurred. Portuguese records of the late fifteenth century and Dutch maps of the early seventeenth century scarcely show any significant changes in the state structure of the coast, which was essentially a kaleidoscope of very many small states, none of which corresponded in size or power with Nigerian states like Oyo or Benin. On the immediate coastline there were at least eight states regarded as important by the early European traders, while behind them, in a second tier of states, lay ten more mentioned as of political significance. With the arrival of Europeans, the two tiers of states began struggling with each other for control of trade routes. On the seashore, each state attempted to enlarge its share of the beach by warfare at the expense of its neighbors. The coastal settlements, at first merely fishing villages, often developed into thriving ports like Sekondi, Kommenda, Cape Coast, Anomabu, and Kormantin, and by the seventeenth century they possessed a class of skilled workers employed by the Europeans as carpenters, builders, cask-makers, and the like, as well as a sizable group of African merchants.

On the coast, however, it would seem that the rivalries between African states produced no radical changes, nor did any one state assume predominance, perhaps because the Portuguese, and later the Dutch, intervened and intrigued to make sure that the Africans remained divided into small political units. Behind the coastline, the second tier of states was more remote from European meddling, and here definite attempts seem to have been made to dominate neighbors east and west, so as to monopolize the routes from the forest to the coast. The area of the Pra and Ofin rivers was first dominated by the state of Twifu, by Adansi after 1550, and then by Assin in the early seventeenth century. By the middle of the seventeenth century Dutch records show that Assin controlled most of the gold trade with the interior. In the eastern area behind the coast there seems to have been a similar pattern, with first Akyem and then Akwamu dominating the interior trade routes. But none of these states, before 1650, was of very large extent.

The entry of Dutch armed traders on the Gold Coast in the seventeenth century was to revolutionize the situation. It has been seen how the Dutch captured Sao Jorge da Mina, made it their headquarters of Elmina, and completely expelled the Portuguese by 1642. During the rest of the seventeenth century the Dutch proceeded to establish almost a dozen posts and forts along the coast, but they were never to enjoy anything like the monopoly once held by the Portuguese, for as the Dutch forts began to dot the coast after 1650, so did those of rival European nations—sometimes practically side by side with each other. With the organization of the Royal African Company in 1672, the English added to their posts at Kormantin (1631) and Winneba (1650) those of Kommenda (1670), Anomabu (1673), Accra (1673), Sekondi (1680), and Dixcove (1691). Other nations came too; in 1652 the Swedes established themselves in Cape Coast, and set up headquarters in Christianborg Castle five years later; between 1685 and 1709 even the electorate of Brandenburg established two forts on the Gold Coast. In such competitive conditions it was impossible to control the trade or restrict the articles of importation, and in this free-for-all arms and ammunition became a major import from Europe. With these more terrifying (if perhaps not much more accurate) weapons it became possible for African states, especially those beyond the pale of immediate European influence, to nurture more grandiose plans of expansion.

The first to succeed were Denkyera, inland from the coast between the Ancobra and Pra rivers, and Akwamu, further east behind Accra. By the end of the century Denkyera controlled most of the inland routes behind the western half of the coast, and had conquered a large extent of territory inland, having subjugated the petty kingdoms of Twifu, Wassaw, Aowin, Assin, and Fetu. Akwamu became a much more extensive state than had yet been seen in the area, controlling the inland states of Kwahu and Akim, pushing eastward across the Volta River to control the canoe traffic, and finally invading the coast itself and subjugating Accra and Agona, thus gaining direct access to the Europeans. Akwamu is also of particular importance as a state in which new administrative techniques were worked out, especially in strengthening the role of kingship, and in reorganizing the structure of the army. The significance of these changes was particularly noticed by the new interior state of Ashanti, and Osei Tutu, the real founder of the Ashanti nation, spent several years as a youth at the Akwamu court, where he absorbed many of the new techniques.

The rise of Denkyera and Akwamu, however, was a mere curtain-raiser to the real revolution in the politics of the Gold Coast which was to come. Between 1690 and 1750 a new pattern emerged in which two power blocs virtually divided the country into two zones —the new nation of Ashanti controlling the inland gold, kola, and products of the rain forest, while the Fante "confederation" grew to place itself between the Ashanti and the Europeans on the sea coast. This pattern of control was to affect profoundly the nature of Gold Coast politics until the establishment of the independent Republic of Ghana.

Ashanti as such had no existence as a state until the late seventeenth century, although its Akan peoples had migrated there from the confluence of the Pra and Ofin rivers much earlier, when they had split off from the main Akan migratory movement. Their object in thus swinging northward was undoubtedly the commercial and economic prospects of the area of what is now Ashanti, for this was not only the chief nearby source of gold and kola nuts, but was also the junction of the two main trade routes from the savannah where the western route from Timbuktu coming down through Jenne and Begho met the route from Hausaland through Gonja. Whoever controlled this junction could monopolize the contact between savannah, forest, and the coastal plain. These early Akan settlements in the area of what was to become Kumasi were, however, excessively fragmented, and even smaller in area than those on the coast at this time.

Unity among them was precipitated by outside aggression. In the middle of the seventeenth century all of them fell under the control of Denkyera, which ruthlessly exploited them as sources of slaves for the growing Dutch and English competition on the coast, monopolized their gold resources, and naturally prohibited them from any contact with the coastal traders. There was a growing hatred for Denkyera domination in all the territories under her control, a hatred fed by Denkyera arrogance which characterized all non-Denkyera as fit only for slavery.

Disaffection, however, was not enough; the subject areas needed leadership to end their disunity, and firearms and ammunition to defeat the well armed Denkyera forces. After 1670 the growth of competitiveness among the Europeans was to provide the arms, while the arrival of a group of late-comers among the Akan was to provide the leadership. This last group was a unified clan named the Oyoko, who founded a number of small states, including Juaben, Kokofu, Nsuta, Bekwai, and Kumasi, all within a few miles of each other. Though originally quite independent units, all these states being of one clan, regarded each other as "brothers" and the possibility of cooperation among them was real. The actual achievement of political unity was the work of a succession of three remarkable rulers of Kumasi, one of the Oyoko clan states.

The first of these, Obiri Yeboa, by the time of his death in the late 1670s, had created a situation in which Kumasi, though still a tiny state, was locally predominant within a radius of some twenty miles. His methods were mainly astute diplomacy, whereby he offered admission to his clan to all the local rulers, thus enlarging the Oyoko group and extending the possible range of cooperation. Those who refused to join he tried to absorb by conquest, and he himself died in battle.

As yet no constitutional unity existed. This was the work of the next Kumasi ruler, regarded by Ashantis as the true founder of their nation, Osei Tutu. Osei Tutu had been "apprenticed" (whether deliberately or not) at the court of Akwamu, and thus absorbed the innovating centralizing tendencies of the south. He brought with him a man who was to be his closest friend and advisor, Okomfo

Anokye. Anokye was a priest and magician, skilled like many African practitioners in the use of his art for political purposes. The Kumasi ruler, advised by Anokye, first worked to forge a military alliance of the local petty states to cooperate against the common foe, Denkyera. Having succeeded, they then proceeded, by the use of magic, to transform the military alliance into a political union. Anokye, we may presume, secretly arranged for the construction of an elaborate golden stool, which was, like the throne in Europe, the symbol of kingship. A great gathering of all the rulers of the alliance was then summoned. At the appropriate moment the golden stool apparently descended from the sky in a black cloud of thunder, to alight near Osei Tutu. The magician then declared that the golden stool embodied the soul of the Ashanti nation, that it was a symbol of their unity, that it must never be lost, and that Osei Tutu and his descendants should possess the golden stool and reign as head of the new nation, and all other existing symbols of authority should be buried.

Presumably the assembled rulers were already predisposed toward a union under Kumasi, or they would not have accepted the magic without protest. Nevertheless, the descent of the golden stool was a masterstroke of theatrical management, for the events, told and retold down to the present day to every Ashanti child, provided exactly the kind of myth needed to cement the new national sense of identity. Anokye went on to create suitable rituals to strengthen further the new state; such as the *odwira* festival, an annual affair in which all *omanhenes* (divisional kings) paid allegiance to the *asantehene* (king of Ashanti) and settled all quarrels among themselves. The festival itself consisted of a kind of purification of the nation, in which thanks were given and prayers said to the gods, and the position of the *asantehene* as the earthly representative of the gods was emphasized.

Beneath these deliberately invented religious sanctions, Osei Tutu and Okomfo Anokye built solid and practical constitutional forms. Kumasi ("magically" chosen by Anokye—perhaps not the most surprising of his many feats!) became the capital city. Osei Tutu assumed the new title of *asantehene* and ruled with the advice of a council composed of the kings (*omanhene*) of all the pre-existing states. These now lost their independent sovereignty, each had to be recognized by the *asantehene*, and this was done only after allegiance to him had been sworn on oath. Each *omanhene* ruled his division conditionally, and could be removed for failing in allegiance to the *asantehene*, for failing to supply troops when asked, for making war against another *omanhene*, or for failure to attend the *odwira* festival. The existence of the nation was symbolized judicially by the right of all freemen to appeal to the *asantehene's* court in Kumasi.

But perhaps the most important of all Osei Tutu's innovations was the structure he gave to the newly created united Ashanti army, making it perhaps the most formidable armed force in the West African forest area. The pre-existing state armies were not simply amalgamated, but each, as a unit, was fitted like a piece of a jigsaw puzzle into a massive new structure. This overall structure was undoubtedly borrowed from Akwamu, and is one of the results of Osei Tutu's apprenticeship there. The army was made up of four divisions, a van, a rear, and left and right wings. Each state army had its alloted place in one of the four positions, and each division was commanded by an *omanhene*. The *mamponhene* (i.e., *omanhene* of Mampon) became commander-in-chief of the whole army, unless the *asantehene* himself decided to go to battle. Every fit Ashanti male was liable for military service.

These armies were soon bloodied; before 1680 they swept against Domaa (who had killed Obiri Yeboa) and forced the Domaas to flee westward and establish the new state of Gyaman (which means "the exiles"). In the 1680s there was a series of wars in and near Kumasi, apparently directed to subduing by force the dissidents who had refused to join the union. These operations were preliminary to the great object, begun in 1699, of throwing off the yoke of Denkyera. By 1701 Ashanti was victorious. Ashanti was now a large and populous state, completely independent.

The victory over Denkyera naturally made the Ashanti conscious of the significance of the European slave trade, and of the presence of the European forts on the coast, for in subduing Denkyera, Ashanti had taken over Denkyera's rights of suzerainty over her southern vassal states, such as Wassaw, Twifu, and Aowin, which lay along the routes to the coast. At the same time Ashanti had taken over the "notes" (i.e., legal titles to the land, for which Europeans paid rent) to the Dutch castle of Elmina. The implications were not immediately apparent, however; for ten years after 1702 Osei Tutu seems to have called a halt to conquest, and pre-occupied himself with digesting the gains. Most of the conquered states were incorporated into the Ashanti union as full members, with their kings reduced to the status of *omanhene,* sometimes with the fall in status sweetened by a judicious marriage alliance with Osei Tutu's family. (The next *asantehene,* Opoku Ware, was in fact an offspring of such a marriage.) Denkyera was defeated but not destroyed. Her continued existence as an independent state al-lowed her to rally her one-time vassals in the south; this provoked further campaigns in the south by Osei Tutu from 1712 to 1716, in the course of which the Ashanti army reached the sea for the first time by taking the port of Appolonia in 1715. In the same year the Dutch, recognizing the new situation, sent a full diplomatic mission under Neyendaal to Kumasi. It would seem that in his last years Osei Tutu was ready to bid for complete supremacy on the coast, not only behind Denkyera, but also in the eastern districts behind Accra, for in 1717 he was killed during operations to suppress re-bellions in Akim.

The sudden abrupt end to Osei Tutu's long reign brought crisis to the Ashanti state, for civil war erupted between rival claimants to the throne. This allowed Denkyera, her vassals, and her allies in Akim and Akwapim to shut out Ashantis from access to the coast once more. By 1720 Opoku Ware had established his position as the third of three great *asantehenes;* his reign was to last until 1750, and was to see the Ashanti state transformed into a territorial empire comparable with those of Oyo and Benin in Nigeria. Though Denkyera and her allies were once again crushed in the 1720s, and trade contacts with the Europeans were resumed, Opoku Ware seems not to have felt the need to establish direct Ashanti rule on any part of the coast at this stage. Instead he turned his attention to the north, extending Ashanti territory up along the trade routes both northwestward on the route to Jenne and Timbuktu, and northeastward toward Gonja and the route to Hausaland. In the course of these conquests important gold-producing areas like Banda and Gyaman were incorporated into the Ashanti union. The wars were extended up into the savannah area, and the Muslim-influenced states of Dagomba, Krachi, and Gonja were brought into subordinate relationships with Ashanti between 1744 and 1746. With these states, perhaps because their cultures were so very different, there was no attempt at incorporation; instead, they were left with compliant native rulers, and forced to pay annual tribute and to send troops when called upon.

Opoku Ware seems to have felt that Ashanti's role lay essentially in northern expansion. This did not, however, mean that the coast remained immune from Ashanti control. In 1730 Akwamu, which had controlled the eastern coastal districts behind Accra for so long, collapsed and was incorporated into Akim. This made Akim, lying between the Ashanti and the key port of Accra, as important as Denkyera had been earlier in the western areas. During a three-year campaign after 1741 the northern wars were temporarily halted, and the Ashanti armies swept south. Akim was defeated and parts of its territories annexed, and the regions of Akwapim, Akwamu, and Ga-Adagbe declared vassal states. In 1744 the Ashanti armies entered Accra itself, where the European traders had two years before begun paying rent for their forts to the *asantehene*. By 1750, therefore, when Opoku Ware died, Ashanti had almost succeeded in creating an empire over most of the territory of the modern Republic of Ghana. The Ashanti Union itself was by far the largest single state, covering almost all of the forest zone. In the north the savannah states of Krachi, Dagomba, and Gonja were tributary, in the south no serious rival could defy Ashanti, and Accra was now a vital outlet to the sea.

Ashanti was not to succeed in forming a single unified state over the whole of Ghana. The check to Ashanti power came from the rise of the Fante, another Akan group closely related to the Ashanti, who eventually formed a state in the south strong and large enough to prevent the Ashanti from securing the whole coastline. The Fante, just like the Ashanti, began as an Akan migrant party from the same original early migration, which separated from the main body and settled at Mankessim, about ten miles inland behind Cape Coast. During the sixteenth and seventeenth centuries parties of colonists moved out from Mankessim and founded as many as twenty new states, many of them little more than independent villages. Some, however, especially those like Anomabu which were on the coast and became slave-trading ports, rose to be considerable towns after 1670. But like the peoples who created the Ashanti nation, the Fante began as disunited and even warring groups, though all attached a certain religious awe to Mankessim, whose chief or *braffo*, as the Europeans called him, was given a sort of token overlordship.

Just as the unification movement in Ashanti had been prompted by the threat of Denkyera, so the Fante began to unite in response to the growing power of Ashanti after 1700. After the defeats of Denkyera the behavior of the Europeans forced the Fante to notice the new importance of Ashanti. After 1700 the English began trying to attract the Ashanti merchants to their posts and interfering in the politics of the interior states to ensure compliant rulers who would allow the Ashanti traders free passage. There were many advantages for England in the emergence of a single power spanning the coast, forest, and edges of the savannah, for it would ensure cheaper prices by reducing the number of middlemen and simplifying the marketing system. Thus, England's attitude not only threatened the commercial position of the Fante, but also spelled political disaster by providing the Ashanti with a sure and independent source of firearms.

These considerations were the driving force behind the movement for Fante unity after 1700. The movement took the form of first building local cooperation among the disunited Fante states, and then of establishing military sway east and west across the routes to the interior. At the same time the Fante secured control of the key seaports of Cape Coast, which was the chief English fort, Elmina (the Dutch headquarters), and Anomabu (an important English trading outlet). The neighboring states were weak and divided, and their ability to resist Fante aggression was further weakened by Dutch and English intrigues in their internal affairs after 1670. The Europeans were naturally not pleased with the rise of a united Fante state, but there was little they could do to stop it, being engaged in the bitter rivalry and open fighting of the Anglo-Dutch wars after the formation of the Royal African Company in 1672. After 1688, with William III, a Dutch king, on the English throne, the two powers were ostensibly close allies, but not in overseas commerce, and where one resisted the Fante, the other allied with them to secure favorable trade concessions.

Despite clear parallels between the Fante and Ashanti movements for unity, and though both states were essentially Akan of the same cultural tradition, the Fante never succeeded in achieving the degree of unity of their rivals. At first sight the Fante state of Abora seemed destined to play the role of Kumasi, but the *braffo* of Abora never became a true king of the whole state. Instead, he was invested with military powers in time of war, but surrounded by a strong parliament composed of delegates from all the states. When the Ashanti armies turned northward after 1720, disunity reappeared among the Fante, and the confederation fell into two sections, an eastern and a western confederation. Nevertheless, the Fante had at least stabilized their position so far as trade was concerned by 1750.

For the rest of the eighteenth century the clash between Ashanti and Fante, which many European observers expected to culminate in a final struggle, failed to materialize, though there were occasional skirmishes. The main reason for the postponement of this trial of strength was a succession of serious internal crises in Ashanti. After the death of Opoku Ware in 1750, the succession of Kusi Obodum was contested, and he was finally deposed in 1764. In 1777 Osei Kwame began his reign as *Asantehene* as a minor, and his supporters needed to crush internal rebellions until about 1790. Thereafter the adult *asantehene* provoked resistance and, finally, revolution by his leanings to Islam. The *omanhenes* were able to see that Islamic ideas of the power of the ruler would seriously reduce their status, and in 1801 they conspired together and destooled (deposed) Osei Kwame. This in turn provoked rebellions in the Muslim states on the northern frontiers which were not suppressed until 1803.

An additional factor delaying the Fante-Ashanti clash, which was to become of supreme importance in the next century, was the development of a British policy of support for the Fante, which emerged after 1765. The British tried to assist the Fante in building alliances and used commercial and diplomatic pressures to dissuade the Ashanti from moving south. The policy was a new development, and represented an abandonment of the earlier reactions to the rise of Ashanti. It was now felt that although an Ashanti hegemony over the coast would possess commercial advantages, its political dangers outweighed all other considerations. The Fante were less united, and one section could always be played off against another;

the Ashanti, on the other hand, would be able to force the British to comply with their wishes by cutting off trade completely if they ever controlled the whole coastline.

The Dutch took much the opposite line, and attempted to use British attitudes to build up a special position of friendliness with Ashanti, keeping the trade route to Elmina open for Ashanti merchants. This guaranteed the arms supply for Ashanti and meant that both sides had the means to fight each other. It seemed that a bid for coastal supremacy would therefore be inevitable once Ashanti's internal problems had settled down, and the nineteenth century was, in fact, dominated by the rivalry of Ashanti and Fante. The Fante were undoubtedly weaker, but the growing power of the British was always enough to balance Ashanti in the last analysis. In these circumstances it was natural that the Fante should come to be influenced more and more by the English language and culture. The Ashanti interior and the Fante-dominated coast, though essentially peopled by the same Akan stock, were divided by history into two rival political and cultural areas. Thus it came about that the rivalry of north and south, which in Nigeria represented real cultural and religious divisions, in Ghana represented a fragmentation of an earlier cultural harmony.

FOUR

THE NINETEENTH CENTURY

Up to the eighteenth century we have seen the evolution of African states in Ghana and Nigeria which met the impact of outside forces without revolutionary change. Neither Islam in the northern areas nor the impact of Europeans in the south fundamentally altered the African traditional bases upon which social and political life depended. In the nineteenth century this situation was completely transformed by the impact of aggressive Islamic revolutionary movements in northern Nigeria and aggressive christian missionary efforts among the coastal and forest kingdoms of southern Ghana and southern Nigeria. Both movements were highly critical of traditional African political and social organization, and each in their different ways attempted to overthrow the old societies and replace them with new religiously orientated systems. As with all religious movements, neither of them was "purely" religious, as political ambitions became inextricably woven into them. The Islamic movement in the north ended by creating a Fulani empire in northern Nigeria, while the Christian missionaries did much to pave the way for British rule in the Gold Coast and southern Nigeria.

The Fulani Jihad in Northern Nigeria

From the fifteenth century onward the Hausa states, as has been seen, were steadily influenced by Islam through contact with merchants and scholars from North Africa and the Middle East, and through more local influences from the great empires like Songhai further west. But this influence was limited, resulting in individual conversions to Islam among ruling families, nobles, merchants, and officials, but not among the farming population of the countryside.

In order to keep control of the masses, Hausa rulers resisted the pressure to bring their political ideology and institutions into line with the Koranic precepts, and heretical practices were widespread. Puritanical and extremist movements developed in several parts of the Muslim world during the eighteenth century. In Arabia Islam was convulsed by the Wahibis, a revolutionary uprising bent on bringing society back to the original purity of the Koran. Similar movements arose in North Africa, and by the late eighteenth century African saints, mystics, and reformers were active in the Senegal area among the Fulani people of Futa Jallon and Futa Toro. From there the new ideas spread to the Fulani of northern Nigeria, who had been infiltrating into the Hausa lands for several centuries. The Fulani immigrants had become divided into two groups—those who remained predominantly a cattle-rearing people, and those who intermarried with the Hausa and established themselves in the towns. These latter became noted as scholars and teachers, and naturally became attracted to political affairs as advisors to several of the Hausa kings. It was from this group that leadership for the coming revolution was to emerge.

By the end of the eighteenth century Gobir, the most northwesterly of the Hausa states, had become the predominant power in Hausaland. In Gobir dwelt the Toronkawa clan of Fulani, who were already noted as something of a missionary clan from the number of teachers and scholars they produced. In the 1770s a young Toronkawa Fulani, Usman dan Fodio, began his career of preaching, first in Gobir, then in Kebbi, after which he spent five years touring Zamfara. By the end of the 1780s Usman was virtually the head of a "movement," and his following was so great that the Hausa king of Gobir attempted to have him assassinated, but failed. The movement continued to grow and spread, and Usman dan Fodio's followers, setting themselves distinctly apart by wearing the turban and the veil, began to call themselves the *jama'a* or community. Usman continued his tours of preaching, attracted a sizable community of scholars to his village of Degel, and began distributing manuscript books and pamphlets in Arabic throughout the Hausa states. His message was still essentially religious, attacking the practices of magic and witchcraft, pagan religious beliefs, superstitions, and the like, but it also had political overtones. Usman attacked the Hausa rulers for perverting Islamic law and levying taxes not sanctioned by the Koran. In 1795, at the significant Muslim age of forty (the age at which Muhamed first had the Koran revealed to him) Usman dan Fodio claimed that he had been instructed in a vision to preach the arming of his followers.

Such a move was bound to alarm the Hausa rulers, especially as it had a particular significance within the context of Islamic political theory. For strict Muslims the world is divided into two parts, the Dwelling of Islam or Peace, and the Dwelling of Darkness. The latter were the non-Muslim countries, and in these places the believer had the duty either to withdraw to a place of Islam or to take up arms against the pagans and offer them the choice of embracing the faith or slavery. But the real difficulty of the doctrine arose over the precise definition of Islam; there clearly came a point, if the practice of Islam was degenerating, when a country passed from Islam to Darkness, in which case the believers had the duty of rebelling to reestablish the faith. Usman's arming of his followers could thus only mean that he was preparing for a total condemnation of Gobir as pagan, and the *jihad* (holy war) would follow.

This was the interpretation which Nafata, the king of Gobir who ascended the throne in 1796, placed upon Usman's movement. He therefore tried to restrict the movement: the wearing of the turban and the veil were declared illegal, the newly converted Muslims were told to recant, and only dan Fodio himself was allowed to preach from that time on. In 1802 Nafata was succeeded as king of Gobir by his son Yunfa, and the new king was even more strongly opposed to Usman—so much so that he attacked the *jama'a* in force. In response Usman emigrated with all his followers into Gudu, outside Gobir territory. This was a significant step, which Usman called the *hijra* after Muhamed's flight on which it was modeled. The believers had fled from the Dwelling of Darkness, and Gobir was now openly condemned as pagan. Followers from other Hausa states now began slowly to trickle into Gudu.

Nafata decided that he could no longer permit the movement to grow outside his borders, from whence it could later invade and destroy him. In June 1804 the Gobir army marched on Usman's followers, who met it at Tabkin Kwotto. Despite inferior numbers, the *jama'a* routed the Gobir army. The *jihad* had begun in earnest. Usman's army began to swell with the aid of Fulani pastoralists, more concerned perhaps with booty than ideals, and disaffected Hausa peasantry anxious to lighten the burden of oppression and taxation. Usman, now known as the *shehu* (sheikh), was repulsed from Gobir itself, but swung his army into Kebbi, which fell in 1805. From there his forces took Gwandu, which now became the headquarters of the movement.

The politically revolutionary character of the movement now became manifest, for the *shehu* began to transform what had begun as a revolt in Gobir into an attempt to unify the whole of northern Nigeria. The Muslim leaders from Katsina, Kano, Daura, and Zamfara were summoned, swore allegiance to the *shehu*, and were given flags and orders to overthrow the Hausa dynasties and establish themselves as *emirs*. The war now spread to every Hausa state, and by 1812 a new empire was in existence, with Fulani *emirs* installed in power, though many of the old Hausa rulers were in hiding or fighting guerilla actions for decades to come. In 1812 Usman dan Fodio, having completed his mission, retired from political life to one of meditation and writing. He divided the empire into two parts, the western half centered on Gwandu with his brother Abdullahi as suzerain *emir*, the eastern section centered on Sokoto with his son Muhamed Bello as sultan and *sarkin musulmi* (commander of the Faithful).

The structure of power was based on an entirely new principle of authority which was essentially a local form of feudalism. The new rulers had no traditional African claim to loyalty, and magical kingship was denied to them by Islam. Their authority was based on the force they could command, on the prestige of Islam, and on the oaths sworn by subordinates. Each local *emir* controlled loyal bodies of cavalry, the leaders of whom were given official positions and functions within the new state, either at the capital, or as chiefs of subordinate towns and villages. The local *emirs* were tied together in two pyramids, the one under Gwandu and the other under Sokoto. The *emir* of Gwandu or the sultan of Sokoto could (and sometimes did) depose recalcitrant *emirs*, and the succession of a new *emir* had to be confirmed by the suzerain. But the unity of the empire was very loose, and almost all the day-to-day affairs of each emirate were in the absolute control of the local *emir*. As the nineteenth century wore on, and the original idealism of the *jihad* evaporated, the authority of Gwandu and Sokoto became less and less, and local *emirs* even made war on each other. Nevertheless, all recognized a single system as existing, and regular correspondence in Arabic passed between the sultan and the *emirs* until the end of the century.

As a Fulani-led movement, the *jihad* might easily have degenerated into the exploitation of one race by another, had not the religious nature of the movement prevented this. Usman's own Toronkawa clan was not "pure" Fulani. (The Fulani are in any case a hybrid Berber-Negro mixture, and the town Fulani had already intermarried with Hausa on a considerable scale.) The wars often divided men more on religious and social than on racial lines. One of the new *emirs* (Yakub of Bauchi) was pure Hausa, and even the Fulani dynasties very rapidly transformed themselves into a Hausa-Fulani aristocracy by intermarriage (intensified by the fact that each *emir* was allowed four legal wives and unlimited concubines). Though political and religious life was refurbished, with Arabic as the written language of government, the Hausa spoken language and urban and rural culture continued.

The Fulani had no intention of confining the *jihad* to the Hausa states. In 1805 Fulani living in the western areas of Bornu rebelled, and new emirates of Katagum and Gombe were thereafter carved out of Bornu territory. In 1808 Fulani armies invaded Bornu and took the capital, forcing the *mai* (king) to flee. Bornu, in fact, had been in a steady decline throughout the eighteenth century, and it seemed as if the empire would collapse. Instead, Bornu found a savior in El Kanemi, leader of the Kanembu emigrants from Kanem. El Kanemi began with a private army, which eventually took over the defeated remnants of the *mai*'s forces and recaptured the capital. Thereafter, despite repeated invasions by the Fulani, El Kanemi rallied Bornu and maintained its territory intact. He became so powerful that in 1814 *mai* Dunama took flight, hoping to collect forces and return to kill El Kanemi, but was captured and deposed. El Kanemi replaced him with a puppet *mai*, no doubt feeling that the traditional divine kingship still had an importance in securing obedience. But the *mai* was now a mere shadow-king, and the real power in the state was exercised by El Kanemi, who took the title of sheik. While stabilizing the troubled frontier with the Fulani's, El Kanemi expanded Bornu eastward, reducing Kanem and Baghirmi, so that it had recovered much of its former medieval splendor by the time of his death. In 1846 El Kanemi's son Sheik Omar, faced with an attempt by the *mai* to resume his authority, abolished the maiship entirely and ended the dynasty.

If Fulani ambitions were frustrated in Bornu they were more successful elsewhere. The Hausa had never really established effective control of the Benue River area, to which the Fulani were attracted by the commercial possibilities, and particularly by their "duty" to subjugate the pagans. The emirates of Gombe and Bauchi began this process; in 1806 Moddibo Adama received the *shehu's* flag and proceeded to found in his own name the emirate of Adamawa, centered on Yola, the farthest point of navigability on the Benue. Farther downstream the emirate of Muri was founded at about the same time. All these states, in what is now the "middle belt," had hitherto experienced little Islamic influence, and their peoples now put up a steady resistance, retreating to the hills. Having thus rejected Islam, they were proper subjects for slave raiding, and the Benue area became thereafter a center for slave supply.

Prolonged guerilla warfare along the Benue prevented any possibility of the Fulani crossing south of the river and pressing through the Ibo areas to the seacoast. There is no doubt that the ambition to "dip the Koran into the Atlantic" was conceived early in the *jihad.* Fulani scholars were far from ignorant of geography, and in the 1820s the English explorers Denham and Clapperton visited Sokoto and discussed the prospects of trade with Britain with Sultan Muhamed Bello. It was not long, therefore, before the Fulani began to press south of the Niger. While the *jihad* was still being waged in Hausaland proper, the Fulani began to intervene in Nupe, the first of the "bastard" states. A civil war, caused by violent quarrels over the succession among members of the Nupe royal family, was in progress in Nupe. The Fulani leader in Nupe, Mallam Dendo, secured a flag from Sokoto, and proceeded to lend Fulani support first to one side and then the other. Though Dendo never declared himself *emir*, he succeeded in using his position as kingmaker to place the Fulani in control and begin the Islamicization of the state.

His death in 1832 was followed by further civil strife, but eventually one of his sons, Masaba, who was born of a Nupe mother, established himself as *emir*.

Nupe territory straddled both sides of the Niger, and was a steppingstone to Fulani intervention in Yorubaland, which was to lead to the complete collapse of the Oyo empire.

The Fall of the Oyo Empire

In the last chapter it was seen that the Oyo empire began to show serious cracks at the end of the eighteenth century, with Dahomey repudiating its tributary status, and the Egba asserting independence. Oyo, the capital, was in the savannah zone, but the impact of European trade had shifted the economic wealth of the empire southward. As the slave trade excited rivalries and commercial jealousies, Oyo began to lose its overall grip. The Fulani now entered the scene to exploit these divisions. In 1817 the *alafin* Aole tried to crush the ambitious Afonja, the *kakanfo* (commander-in-chief) who was also governor of Ilorin, which lay southwest of Nupe where the Fulani had already made inroads. Aole's expedient was the time-honored Yoruba ruse of ordering *kakanfo* Afonja to attack an impregnable town, knowing that failure entailed the traditional obligation for the *kakanfo* to commit suicide. Afonja, however, sensed the plot, and had the *alafin's* messengers who brought the order murdered. Then, with the support of other dissident chiefs, he sent Aole the customary empty calabash, indicating that it was he who should commit suicide. Aole was traditionalist enough to accept defeat, but before killing himself he prophesied that the Yoruba nation would be carried away as slaves and that slaves would rule over them. This was indeed a remarkably accurate description of the coming history of the Yoruba for the rest of the century, for the Oyo empire was about to collapse in a welter of civil war and internecine fighting; Yoruba would enslave Yoruba and sell them overseas, and liberated slaves would eventually return to become rulers.

Afonja used the opportunity of Aole's suicide to declare Ilorin independent, and better to defy the new *alafin* he called in Fulani help, in the person of Mallam Alimi, a noted local Fulani scholar. Alimi brought in Fulani and Hausa soldiers to defeat the invading armies of the new *alafin* of Oyo, who in turn committed suicide.

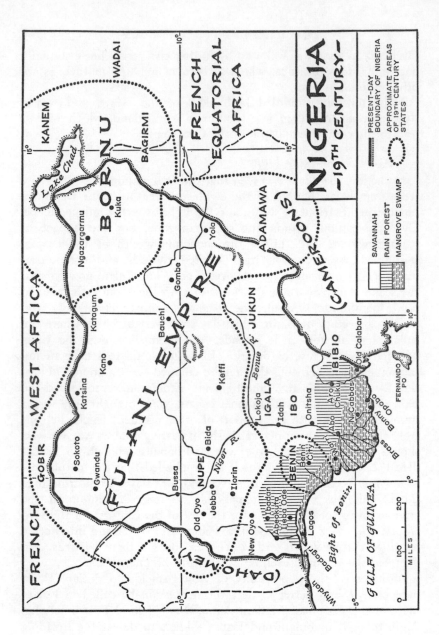

NIGERIA
—19TH CENTURY—

PRESENT-DAY
BOUNDARY OF NIGERIA
APPROXIMATE AREAS
OF 19TH CENTURY
STATES

SAVANNAH
RAIN FOREST
MANGROVE SWAMP

WADAI

KANEM

BORNU

BAGIRMI

FRENCH EQUATORIAL AFRICA

Ngazargarmu

Lake Chad

Kuka

WEST AFRICA

ADAMAWA

Yola

GOBIR

Katagum

Bauchi

Gombe

JUKUN (CAMEROONS)

Kano

Katsina

Keffi

Benue R.

IGALA

IBIBIO

Old Calabar

FULANI EMPIRE

Lokoja

Idah

IBO

Onitsha

Aro Chuku

N.Cabbass

FERNANDO PO

Sokoto

Gwandu

Bida

NUPE

Niger R.

Aboh

Opobo

FRENCH

Bussa

Ilorin

Old Oyo

Jebba

New Oyo

BENIN CITY

Ibadan

Abeokuta

Ijebu Ode

Lagos

Bonny

Brass

(DAHOMEY)

Badagri

Bight of Benin

GULF OF GUINEA

Whydah

MILES
0   100   200

106

Mallam Alimi, like Mallam Dendo in Ilorin, preferred to work through Afonja and never seized open control, but when Alimi died in 1832, his son Abdusallami defeated Afonja's forces in open battle, killed Afonja, and burned his body in the market place. Abdusallami thus became the first *emir* of Ilorin, and this Yoruba state became part of the Fulani empire. To this day it forms part of the northern region of Nigeria, despite the fact that its people are Yoruba.

The defection of Ilorin under Afonja in 1817 led to a rapid and catastrophic disintegration of Oyo control in all its provinces. By 1822 the *alafin* actually ruled only the city of Oyo and the immediately surrounding lands. Though still regarded as a figure of great prestige, not without sentimental value as a symbol of Yoruba culture, the *alafin* had lost almost all power as the Yoruba towns abandoned any pretence of obeying his administration. Each Yoruba town, under its now independent *oba*, looked only to its own interest and advantage. The Fulani control of Ilorin stopped the Yoruba from raiding north for slaves, and they began to look to each other as sources of slave supply. In the process they lost all sense of common Yoruba objectives, and the country fell into an almost permanent state of internecine warfare for the next eighty years, with only short and unstable periods of uneasy truce. There was no attempt to combine against Ilorin and the Fulani menace, and Ilorin was even able to find allies among the Yoruba towns. The details of the long series of wars and the incidents which led to the outbreak of each are too complex to discuss here, but in general it may be said that until 1840 the only power to make gains from the chaos was Ilorin. After 1835 Ilorin influence was strong even in Oyo itself, and the *emir* of Ilorin made a serious effort to try to force the *alafin* to become a Muslim. This prompted Oyo to a desperate and final bid to throw off the threat from Ilorin and reconquer it from the Fulani by calling in the help of Borgu, once Oyo's vassal. The result for Oyo was disaster, the allied armies were utterly defeated, and the Ilorin army took Oyo, which they destroyed completely and ploughed up the site, as the Romans had done when they sacked Carthage. The Oyo were forced to evacuate their territories *en masse*, and to migrate out of the savannah area to settle much further south and build a new Oyo on the fringes of the forest.

The astonishing thing is really that the Yoruba managed to survive at all, for not only were they menaced from the north by Ilorin and the Fulani, but after 1818 their one-time vassals the Dahomey began invading from the west. No pan-Yoruba alliance was ever forged to meet these threats on two fronts, yet the invaders were checked, though never destroyed. That the Yoruba were able to do this was the result of a combination of factors.

Firstly, in meeting the Fulani challenge, geography became an ally of the Yoruba after the destruction of Old Oyo. Oyo, Ilorin, and the northern areas of Yorubaland now under Fulani control lay in the savannah grasslands and were ideal country for cavalry operations. Once the Fulani cavalry began to move into the rain forest, however, the Yoruba found a useful ally in the tsetse fly which brought death to the horses, so that even short raids by cavalry were not easy in the wooded country. Secondly, the Yoruba began to rely increasingly on firearms, the spread of which was a result of the intensification of the slave trade produced by the wars. Arms and ammunition began to be imported on an increasingly large scale, and they were of much more use to infantry or beleagured town garrisons than to the mounted Fulani and Hausa troops, who did not become skilled in their use before 1900.

In the last analysis, armies were needed to check the northern advance, and these were finally provided by the foundation and growth of the city of Ibadan, the most rapid and populous urban development in the whole history of pre-colonial tropical Africa. In the first decade of the nineteenth century Ibadan was a small village of no particular significance, with a fine defensive position on a hillside topped by rocky outcrops. In 1829 a mixed party of refugees from Ife, Egba, Ijebu, and Oyo decided to settle there for defensive reasons. They were soon quarreling among themselves, and in 1830 the Egba contingent moved out to settle further south and establish Abeokuta, which, as will be seen, was to play much the same role in containing the threat of Dahomey as Ibadan did against the Fulani. Thereafter Ibadan established its own forms of civil government, and began to build up its army, still mainly a defensive instrument. When Old Oyo fell in 1837, the site of New Oyo was deliberately chosen so as to be close to Ibadan, by this time a town of several thousand Yoruba who had been attracted there by its security from many parts of the country. The city was unique in that at this stage it was an urban concentration of farmers, with little trade except the all-important exchange of slaves for arms and ammunition. The people lived in the city for security against attack, and often traveled ten or twenty miles daily to their farms. With the foundation of New Oyo under Ibadan's shadow, the *alafin* appointed the ruler of Ibadan *basorun* (war chief) of the "imperial" forces, and gave Ibadan the duty of protecting the northeast frontiers against the Fulani. In 1840 the Ibadan army took the field against Ilorin and obtained a decisive victory by relieving the besieged town of Oshogbo. This was the first check to the Fulani advance, and in the long run proved to be decisive, for the Fulani were never able to advance further into Yorubaland.

The British Anti-Slavery Movement and the "Return of the Exiles"

Before discussion of the way in which Abeokuta, the newly founded Egba state, succeeded in protecting the western frontiers of Yorubaland against the Dahomeyan invasion, it is necessary to examine the profound change which had come over British policy and attitudes since 1800, for British influence and the forces of protestant missionary Christianity now began to play a part in southern Nigeria and southern Ghana comparable in many ways to the *jihad* of the Muslims in the north.

The rise of evangelical protestantism in England had profound effects on Africa. From the earliest days of their movement, evangelists had been aware of the implications of their doctrines, which presupposed a basic human equality before God, for non-European peoples. By the end of the eighteenth century the evangelical churches were beginning to send missionaries to the Negro slaves of the West Indies. Though normally conservative and apolitical, the missionaries there soon discovered that it was impossible, because of the system of slavery, for Negroes to behave as "proper" Christians. A man could not be a good father if his children were liable to be sold away from him, nor sexually moral when his owner forbade him to marry, nor cover his "disgusting nakedness" when he received no wages. The missionaries gradually came to the conclusion, therefore, that slavery must be the work of the devil, for it was clearly an institution designed to prevent the spread of the Gospel and the Christian life. When they turned to examine the state of Africa they came to much the same conclusion; their English middle-class values were disgusted by the nakedness, polygamy, dirt, disease, worship of "idols," and prevalence of superstition. Africa was indeed the "dark continent," and the cause of all this misery was the curse of the slave trade.

Others before them had attacked the trade, especially the Quakers, but they had had no success while the trade and the sugar plantations of the West Indies had formed the backbone of the imperial economy. Now, however, the cold reasoning of the economists was added to the violent emotionalism of the "saints." Had not the industrial revolution showed that "laisser faire" was the best system of all? Labor was a commodity like goods, and a proper economic organization demanded that the laborer sell his labor to the highest bidder. Slavery was artificial and unnatural, it ignored the role of supply and demand, it gave no incentive to the worker except the whip. "Work done by slaves," declared Adam Smith, "is in the end the dearest of all." Moreover, slavery destroyed the Negro as a customer, it gave him no purchasing power through wages, thereby eliminating vast markets for Lancashire cotton cloth, Birmingham hardware, and the other mass manufactures of Britain. The slave trade in Africa similarly destroyed true commerce by exporting labor which would otherwise produce surpluses there which could be traded for British goods.

The anti-slavery movement was thus a unique blend of emotional and religious fervor and cold economic advantage, which was both noble and culturally arrogant. The driving force, however, lay with the "saints," the small group of Quakers and evangelicals like Thomas Clarkson and William Wilberforce who directed the political fight for abolition. The movement soon had repercussions in Africa. In 1772 the Quaker Granville Sharp secured a judgment from Lord Chief Justice Mansfield that there was no positive law in England which countenanced slavery. At one stroke all British Negroes were freed. Clarkson then began to develop the plan of founding a colony of freed Negroes in West Africa, where the slave trade and slavery would be illegal, the object of which would be to convince the surrounding African peoples of the superiority of a free way of life and "legitimate commerce." In 1787 the Sierra Leone Company began operations, and Freetown came into existence.

In 1807 Wilberforce's motion to abolish the slave trade finally secured Parliamentary assent, and the slave trade became illegal for British subjects. At the same time the faltering and bankrupt Sierra Leone Company was taken over by the Crown, and Freetown made the base for the Royal Navy squadron detailed to patrol the West African coast and search for slavers. The 1807 Act was followed by a steady diplomatic activity, in which the British negotiated with other European powers to concede the right for Royal Navy ships to search their ships on the high seas and arrest foreign slavers.

The anti-slavery policy was never purely one of simple repression, for the humanitarian theory stressed from the first the concept that final victory over the slave trade could only come when Africans themselves ceased the trade, and that in order to bring this about Africans needed to be provided with an alternative moral and religious system. It was natural that Britain should offer evangelical protestantism and free trade, and that she should equate these two as "civilization." Christianity, Commerce, and Civilization thus became the watchwords of British policy in Africa. Colonization, however, was not added to the slogan. Colonies were attacked by free trade theorists as useless and expensive encumbrances, artificial and unsuccessful as stimulants of trade, and particularly undesirable in West Africa where disease carried away officials by the score. Instead, Britain was urged to build up and strengthen "good" African rulers who cooperated in fostering legitimate commerce, and to use her influence—and even naval force—against "bad" rulers who persisted in the slave trade and obstructed missionaries.

Despite the deliberate attempt to eschew colonial ventures, the British policy was a revolutionary change in Afro-European relations. Hitherto contact had been completely coastal, and relations passive. The policy of legitimate commerce was active: it deliberately aimed at securing a complete change in the internal economies of African states, and regarded Christian proselytizing as a means to that end. It looked not simply to the coasts, whose African slave-trade middlemen would obviously be reluctant to abandon their livelihoods, but to the interior, to the areas of slave supply, where it was hoped new crops for export like cotton would arise to replace slaves and at the same time feed British industry, create local purchasing power, and provide markets for exports.

One of the first effects of this new set of attitudes was the growth of geographical exploration from 1790 onward. If legitimate commerce was to be fostered it was necessary to map out the broad shape of the inland areas, to plot the internal routes and extent of the slave trade, to find out what legitimate export commodities could be produced inland and what British exports would be acceptable, and above all to find methods of bringing trade to the interior in an area where the tsetse fly prevented horse-drawn wheeled traffic. The plotting of river courses, especially after the development of the steamship in the 1820s, naturally became the focus of interest, and this in turn drew the explorers to the savannah zone, where the existence of the inland Niger River had been known since classical times while its outlet to the sea remained a mystery. Once the explorers began to wander in the savannah areas they began to create exaggerated hopes and optimistic prejudices, for here they come across Africans whose social and political organization much more closely resembled that of Europe, unlike those of the coast. Their centralized states, standing armies, Muslim religion, literacy, and systems of taxation were all recognizable to Europeans as "civilization"; moreover, they wore voluminous cotton robes, and here was a splendid opportunity for Lancashire exports! The picture began to emerge of a benighted and barbarous coast, shutting off the civilized interior from contact with Europe and "progress."

The years from 1807 to 1830 were, however, extremely disappointing. The explorations of Denham, Clapperton, and Lander in the Fulani empire in the 1820s gave promise of great prospects, but these explorers had reached northern Nigeria across the Sahara, an impractical route for British commerce, and the problem of the Niger's sea outlet remained unsolved. Worst of all, the slave trade, far from being reduced by the Royal Navy's patrols, actually increased. Brazil and Cuba were both hungry for slaves for their rapidly expanding sugar and coffee plantations, and the southern United States was pushing its cotton economy ever westward. Though the Danes had actually abolished their trade before the British, and the Dutch followed suit, Portuguese, French, and Spanish ships evaded treaty restrictions, and the United States would never agree to permit her ships to be searched. Brazilians now entered the trade in large numbers, and the Yoruba wars made Lagos, Porto Novo, and Whydah magnets for their ships.

On the Gold Coast the abolition of the British slave trade practically led to a withdrawal of the British presence by 1830, the culmination of a series of disasters. After 1807 the British forts, administered since 1750 by the slave-trading Company of African Merchants, seemed to lose their *raison d'être*. As the Danes and Dutch also abolished slaving, that trade fairly quickly died, but no thriving legitimate trade rose to take its place, except for a little gold and a trickle of palm oil. Relations with the coastal states were seriously injured by abolition, for they could see no reason for the sudden *volte face*. The Company of African Merchants was ineffective, near bankrupt, and suspected by humanitarians because of its history of slaving. Worse still, abolition came at a time of acute crisis in the affairs of the Gold Coast, for in 1806 the Ashanti attacked the Fante in strength, for defying the *asantehene* by harboring political fugitives from his court. The Ashanti army met the Fante at Abora, only four miles from the coast, and completely defeated it. Torrane, the British commander, after supporting the Fante, was ignominiously forced by the Ashanti to surrender political refugees, to allow the Ashanti to enslave British allies, and to agree to the payment of rent for British coastal forts to Ashanti.

The Ashanti victory was not permanent, however, for smallpox struck their armies and forced them to return home in 1807. Thereafter the Fante began again to re-arm and pull the other coastal states together in a desperate alliance. They thus succeeded in checking another Ashanti invasion of 1811, and in further campaigns of 1814-16, although the Ashanti virtually occupied the coast, the Fante and allied forces remained in action and fought steady guerilla actions. The Ashanti now regarded the Fante and all the coastal states as Ashanti territory, but the Fante rejected this assertion. Meanwhile trade was virtually at a standstill.

The British Government and Parliament were becoming increasingly restive with the failure of the Company of African Merchants to resolve this situation. In 1819 the British sent a government representative, Joseph Dupuis, to negotiate directly with the *asantehene* in Kumasi, and in 1821 Parliament abolished the Company entirely, and placed the forts under the control of the Governor of Sierra Leone, Sir Charles Macarthy. Macarthy was a partisan of the humanitarian cause, his sympathies lay with the Fante, and he regarded the Ashanti as savages and slave hunters. When the Ashanti kidnapped and killed a British African policeman from Anomabu who had insulted the *asantehene's* name, Macarthy resolved to crush Ashanti, and thought that he could do it with the five hundred regular troops at his disposal and the aid of Fante allies. He was sorely mistaken. The Ashanti struck the coast in 1824, caught Macarthy with his forces divided, and killed him and most of his troops at Bonsaso. Though the British were later revenged by defeating yet another Ashanti invasion of the coast in 1826, the defeat and death of Macarthy demonstrated to the British government that the best policy was to withdraw from the Gold Coast entirely. This decision was opposed by the British traders, and the government finally compromised with them by allowing a committee of merchants to take over the administration of the forts, and paying them a small annual subsidy. This was done in 1828, and the British government withdrew its officials.

The general pattern of British failure was relieved by one outstanding success for "legitimate commerce." This was in the Niger delta, whose city-states had been the greatest center of the slave trade in the eighteenth century. By the end of the century the traders of Liverpool had engrossed most of the delta slave trade, and the abolition act of 1807 was at first a severe blow to them, allowing Portuguese and Brazilian ships to take over. Soon, however, the more enterprising Liverpool traders were finding a substitute in palm oil, made from crushing the fruit of the Guinea palm which grew in profusion in the rain forests behind the delta. Palm oil was useful not only for lubricating the machinery of industrial Lancashire, but was also an essential ingredient in soap—once an article used only by the rich, but now being mass-produced for dirty British industrial workers. The center of the soap industry lay in Cheshire, not more than twenty miles from the port of Liverpool. From a trickle in 1807 palm oil imports to Britain rose to be worth one million pounds a year in the 1840s. The palm oil trade did not mean that the slave trade ceased, for states like Bonny and Brass dealt impartially with the

British for oil and the Brazilians for slaves. But by the 1830s the extent and profitability of the oil trade, especially in Calabar, was leading to a situation in which African middlemen were beginning to abandon export slave trading as less profitable. By this time the area had become known as the "Oil Rivers."

Then in 1830 came a sudden and dramatic solution to the problem of the Niger mouth. Richard Lander, who had accompanied Clapperton as his valet in his journeys to northern Nigeria, set off overland to the known upper reaches of the great river, purchased canoes and stores, and simply allowed the river's flow to carry him down to the sea. He emerged at Brass to discover that the Oil Rivers hitherto thought to be distinct rivers, were in fact delta mouths of the Niger. This discovery fired the imagination of the Liverpool shipbuilder Macgregor Laird, who, acting in concert with Lander, determined to use the discovery to begin inland trade, experimenting with a specially constructed iron steamship, the first to make a complete ocean voyage. In 1832-34 Laird ascended the Niger as far as Nupe, but the venture was disastrous. One-third of the Europeans engaged died from disease and Laird vowed never to enter the Niger again until the health problem was solved. The Liverpool traders in the Oil Rivers, operating through their African middlemen, had opposed the venture, fearing the competition of direct inland traders, and their stand seemed triumphantly vindicated. Private traders were to keep out of the Niger until the 1850s.

Thus by the 1830s attempts to move inland had been seriously checked; the Ashanti victories had almost led to the abandonment of the Gold Coast and Niger penetration had come to a halt. It was now the humanitarians and the missionary movement which was to continue the inland movement. In order to understand the way in which this inland missionary movement developed, it is important to realize that its impetus came not simply from missionary enthusiasm in Britain, but also from active pressure from a newly formed class of Africans. In fact, the humanitarians in Britain were fully preoccupied before 1838 in fighting for the abolition of slavery in the West Indies and for the rights of Bushmen and Hottentots in South Africa (where the Dutch Cape Colony had been annexed in the Napoleonic wars).

The African pressures arose from the situation in Freetown, Sierra

Leone, where the slave ships captured by the Royal Navy off the West African coast were taken and their human cargoes released. These Africans were of practically all the peoples of West Africa, but a sizable group were the product of the Yoruba wars. Hitherto such people had known only their own villages or towns and its immediate areas; they had obeyed the customs of their people by force of habit and custom, accepted traditional religious beliefs knowing no other, regarded themselves as decent human beings and all strangers and foreigners as savages and barbarians. The experience of capture, enslavement, and sale to the slave ships, with many of the slaves believing that they would be eaten as meat by the white men, were enough to drive lesser men insane. But then to be fired on by other white men, "captured" again, have the shackles removed, and be taken to Sierra Leone and released was, if more pleasant, a puzzling and provocative experience. In Freetown the liberated Africans were "resettled," often passing through missionary hands, and many of their children were put to school. The whole experience of capture and release was bound to shake the very foundations of their beliefs and customs. The liberated Africans were forced to distinguish between white men, labeling some "bad" and some "good." It was natural that they should regard the culture and religion of their British liberators with interest, and that some should imitate it. To make a living in Sierra Leone they had to learn rudimentary English. They were forced to live cheek by jowl with men of tribes they had never heard of before, and to observe that all Africans did not have the same customs, and to consider whether their own were so perfect as they had believed. In the cosmopolitan city of Freetown, dominated by its creole English-speaking free Negroes, they could quickly see that education and literacy were the key to wealth and success, and that the Christian missionaries with their schools could offer that key.

At the same time the "exiles" were homesick, as were all Africans torn from their families and clans. The most numerous group, the Yoruba, began making communal efforts to regain contact with their homeland. They began forming syndicates to purchase captured slave ships condemned by the Freetown slave court—ships which were purified with new names like the *Wilberforce*. With these they began trading down the coast as far as Badagry and Lagos. Here they gathered information and began to piece together the political situation in Yorubaland. It was clear that Badagry and Lagos might be good places to settle, for they were on the coast and within call of the Royal Navy, but in the interior there was also an inviting prospect—Abeokuta.

Abeokuta, as was seen, was an offshoot of the Ibadan settlement. It was founded in 1830 by the Egba group, together with other refugees from the Yoruba wars, led by Sodeke. Its site was chosen for its excellent defensive position, lying under the shadow of huge and high rocky outcrops which dominated the surrounding countryside, but it also had a vital strategic position, lying south of Ibadan halfway along the route to Lagos and the sea. Now that Dahomey had thrown off any Yoruba control and was actively hostile, the Yoruba, including Ibadan, could no longer rely on using Porto Novo or Whydah to obtain arms and ammunition and sell slaves, and Lagos, now only theoretically under Benin, became the Yoruba outlet. Abeokuta thus controlled one of the two major routes from Lagos to Ibadan. (The other lay further east through Ijebu.) Both Ibadan and Ijebu tried to crush the infant Egba state in the 1830s, but the rock was impregnable.

Abeokuta established an *ad hoc* system of conciliar rule, with the chiefs of all districts sitting together. But Sodeke retained executive leadership, strengthened by perpetual external threats. Sodeke realized that Abeokuta needed all the skills, talents, and assistance available to her in order to survive. When *Saro* (an Egba corruption of "Sierra Leonean," i.e., Yoruba from Freetown) made contact with him through Lagos, he let it be known that such friends of the white man would be welcomed. Such an attitude was itself an indication of the change which had come over Yoruba attitudes in the chaos of the wars, for the *Saro* were ex-slaves, and would normally have been objects of derision and scorn to the freeborn.

In the 1830s organized groups of Yoruba from Freetown began moving back to their homeland, settling at Lagos and Abeokuta. The Lagos group at first fared badly, being robbed of all their goods. The Abeokuta settlers remained for a time in Badagry, where some stayed, but the majority of about five hundred later moved on to Abeokuta, where Sodeke welcomed them. Once there the *Saro* began to show their radical tendencies. They were soon influential as military advisors, most of them having picked up a useful knowledge of firearms and British military organization. Many became traders, with useful contacts in Freetown. They were not content with things as they were and began suggesting major innovations in society. They were contemptuous of many ancient customs, and Sodeke agreed that they did not need to prostrate themselves before him like ordinary citizens. At the same time the Christians among the *Saro* had already begun to organize themselves as a distinct group, and to make contact with Freetown requesting missionaries.

These requests came at a time of renewed humanitarian interest in West Africa. The Great Trek of the Boer population in South Africa removed the most intransigent opposition to liberal policies toward Africans in Cape Colony; in 1833 slavery had been abolished in British territories overseas, and in 1838 its last vestige in the system of apprenticeship had been destroyed by humanitarian attacks in parliament. Almost immediately Thomas Fowell Buxton, successor to Wilberforce as leader of the British humanitarians, turned his attentions to West Africa, where he was appalled to discover that the slave trade was actually on the increase despite the naval blockade. In 1840 he published *The African Slave Trade and its Remedy*, in which he refurbished the old idea of the "positive" policy of legitimate commerce by putting forward a scheme for a government sponsored expedition to the Niger, which would make treaties with the local riverain rulers in which they agreed to abandon the slave trade and receive compensation in the form of legitimate commerce. Agricultural experts would be settled at Lokoja, the confluence of the Niger and Benue rivers, there to set up a model farm to teach Africans to grow cotton and other crops, and detailed reports would be made of the economic prospects, desire for missionaries, and languages of the riverain peoples. The humanitarian influence was at its height, and in 1841 the British government accepted the plan.

Laird and other experienced traders had warned of the dangers to health, but the 145 Europeans on the expedition were sanguine in the knowledge that they were engaged in God's work. The result was disastrous; forty-eight of them were dead within two months of entering the Niger, and every white man on the expedition went down with fever. The humanitarians were discredited in Britain, and attacked in the newspapers as irresponsible optimists. The penetration of the Niger was delayed for over a decade.

Nevertheless, although not realized at the time, the failure of the 1841 expedition was to have important effects upon African attitudes among the ex-slave groups. The 1841 expedition had engaged as a linguist Samuel Ajayi Crowther, a man destined to play a dominant role in the nineteenth-century development of Nigeria. Crowther was a Yoruba, seized during the Yoruba wars in the 1820s, but released by the navy and liberated in Freetown. There his powerful intellect attracted the attention of a missionary couple who adopted him, and in 1825 he became a Christian. He was then sent to school in London, and returned to Freetown as a schoolteacher. Already an expert in classical languages, he turned these talents to the study of West African languages, and began constructing their academic grammars; it was this work which brought him to the British government's attention.

Crowther accomplished nothing linguistically on the 1841 expedition—he was constantly kept busy tending the sick and dying, and even stoking the engines between times. The experience was appalling, and convinced him that white men could achieve nothing in the interior. He himself remained healthy, as did most of the African crew on the expedition, and this convinced him that resistance to disease was a racial trait of Negroes. He resolved to become a priest himself, and to work as an interior missionary, not only to work for his race, but also to prevent the useless waste of white lives. He returned to London for further study, and was ordained a priest of the Church of England in 1843.

Thus was born the concept of "African agency," which was of far more than purely religious significance. Hitherto, liberated Africans had been essentially imitators, willing to follow and receive help. Now, with a growing body of African clergy bent on the "regeneration" of Africa to lead them, they became an active force, revolutionary in intent. As the African clergy rose to fame and respected status, education became even more a symbol of status, and liberated Africans chafed even more against traditional restrictions.

The missionary advance into West Africa in the 1840s thus became not merely a British response to African demand, but an Afro-European movement. Unknown to Crowther, he was part of a general world-wide resurgence and activism among Negroes, and the myth of Negro racial immunity to African disease began to bring non-African Negroes also. Thomas Birch Freeman, the English son of a Negro father and a European mother, was prompted to become ordained by the appalling death rate of Wesleyan missionaries on the Gold Coast, and it was he who responded first to the appeal of the Saro in Abeokuta, establishing missions in Badagry and Abeokuta in 1842. As soon as Crowther was ordained in 1843 the Church (of England) Missionary Society (CMS) posted him, along with two white missionaries, in Abeokuta. Here Sodeke had died, and the mission began with difficulty; persecutions broke out in 1848 over Christian burials, which were offensive to traditional beliefs. But in 1851, when Dahomey invaded Abeokuta, the Christian group reached the high point of its influence. The missionaries became the chief military advisors of the Egba state, the British sent arms and military supplies, and the formidable Dahomey army was defeated at the gates of the city. Abeokuta now began to assume special significance in Britain; prayers for its safety were said in English churches, the royal family sent gifts to the chiefs, and Crowther was received in audience by queen Victoria on his next leave to England.

In the Oil Rivers area Negroes also played a part in the establishment of Christian groups. Here the presbyterians established themselves at Calabar in 1846 under the leadership of Hope Waddell, whose staff was a Christian Negro group from Jamaica. The mission very quickly established a strong political influence, supported by ex-slaves, and strengthened by the fear of slave rebellion among the rulers. A reformist spirit soon began to manifest itself, and in 1850 the ruling Ekpe secret society itself enacted a law that human sacrifice should cease.

The Niger Mission

The fullest and most significant development of the concept of "African agency" was to come on the Niger river. In 1854 Laird returned to mount another trading expedition up the river, convinced that the surgeon W. B. Baikie had found the answer to the health problem. The British government encouraged the move, for it had sent Dr. Barth, the greatest of all African explorers, over the Sahara to northern Nigeria, hoping that he could be brought back down the Niger. Baikie's expedition, though failing to link up with Barth, was a triumph; by administering daily doses of quinine to his men he returned without a single death. Moreover, the expedition made a trading profit. Laird's steamship company now received a subsidy to open up trade, and from this time forward British steamers began a regular commerce on the Niger.

Crowther accompanied the 1854 expedition, planning sites for a Niger mission. With the full backing of the CMS he proceeded, after 1857, to establish a chain of mission stations along the Niger right up to the Muslim state of Nupe, staffed entirely by African clergy, most of them trained in Sierra Leone. Though there was opposition to this from white missionaries in Yorubaland, Crowther was supported by Henry Venn, the lay secretary of the CMS, and in 1864 Crowther was raised to the purple as the first African to become an Anglican bishop. The political overtones of the Niger mission were very pronounced; indeed, it is here that we can detect the first stirring of Nigerian nationalism. Crowther and his clergy were were determined to demonstrate "the capacity of the Negro race." They were virtually independent in their organization, and their achievements could not be put down to white supervision. Moreover, though Crowther and several of his clergy were Yoruba, they completely lacked a sense of "tribalism," dedicating their lives to work among Ibo, Ijo, Igala, and Nupe. By fixing on the Niger River they began to visualize a new nation, spanning across tribal divisions, with the great Niger transport system as its heart. The management of the Niger Church was seen as a training ground of responsibility in self-government, designed through its schools to produce a new generation of citizens with wider views and progressive horizons. At the same time, it was realized that this new nation could only come about by outside interference, and all their prejudices led them to hope that it would be the British who would intervene. Thus, paradoxically, these early "nationalists" were also "imperialists," and in later years many of them, including Crowther, would actively assist the British to establish colonial rule.

The Growth of British Political Influence

Although the concept of "legitimate commerce" envisaged development through missions and trade, without colonial rule, it was inevitable that, as the influence of missionaries and traders moved more and more inland, the British government would be increasingly implicated in African politics. The traders and missionaries, whether whites from Britain, or liberated Africans from Sierra Leone, were British subjects, and could demand protection for their legal activities. The more their efforts succeeded and spread further afield, the more complex became their relationships with African states, and the more likely were disputes.

This tendency first showed itself in the Gold Coast. The Committee of Merchants which took over the administration of the forts in 1828 found a most able administrator in George Maclean, who arrived on the coast in 1830. The cornerstone of Maclean's policy was the peace which he negotiated with Ashanti in 1831, in which the Ashanti renounced their claim to control the coastal forts. Maclean could see that it was essential to restore peace and stability to the coastal area and to allow the Ashanti sure communication with the coast for their trade in order to keep them quiet in the future. Though he possessed no constitutional authority to do so, Maclean proceeded to establish a network of judicial procedures, welcomed by most of the coastal states, designed to settle disputes between them and to keep trade moving. Those who refused to co-operate he attacked with his own meager police and African allies and forced them into compliance. As a result, trade increased five times in the ten years after 1831.

Nevertheless, the whole policy was based on shaky foundations, for Maclean had no legal authority behind his measures. He had personal enemies in Britain willing to exploit this situation, and in 1841 and 1842 Parliament instituted inquiries into his regime. The 1842 inquiry praised Maclean's work, but admitted that much of what he had done was strictly illegal. It recommended that the British government return to the Gold Coast, and place its authority on a proper basis by treaties with the coastal states.

In 1843 Parliament passed the Foreign Jurisdiction Act, a curious legal document which allowed the Crown to assume jurisdiction in a foreign territory in as full a manner as if that territory had been ceded as a colony. The Gold Coast forts were placed under a lieutenant-governor, and in 1844 many of the coastal rulers were induced to sign papers passing over judicial powers to the Crown. Maclean was made judicial assessor and his work was thus "legalized." Through these "Bonds" a curious situation had emerged, in which Britain, while not claiming any colonial authority in the coast, nevertheless claimed a supreme judicial control.

In 1849 the palm oil trade in the Oil Rivers had become so valuable that the British government appointed John Beecroft as consul. This in itself was a normal development of relations with independent states, but Beecroft was to make more of his position than mere diplomacy might warrant, arrogating to himself the position of a final arbiter in the affairs of the area. Almost immediately he was securing the deposition of King William Pepple of Bonny, deciding succession questions in Calabar, and decisively intervening in the domestic affairs of Lagos. The Lagos question is an interesting illustration of the way in which missionaries were beginning to involve the British government. In 1845 the king of Lagos, Akitoye, had been overthrown by his nephew Kosoko. Both men were in fact implicated in the slave trade, but Kosoko proved himself unfriendly to Abeokuta. Akitoye naturally wished to collect whatever support he could for his cause, and therefore gave the missionaries in Abeokuta to understand that he was an opponent of the slave trade, who would open up the routes to Abeokuta if restored to power. The missionaries therefore pressed the British government to act, painting a picture of Kosoko as a "wicked slaver" and Akitoye as an enlightened progressive ruler. In 1851 Beecroft intervened and deposed Kosoko. Naturally Akitoye and his son Docemo, who succeeded him, virtually became British puppets. Kosoko fled along the coast and waited his chance to return; he had a sizable body of supporters in Lagos, and the British were forced to secure Akitoye and Docemo by constant support. By 1861 the British were merely regularizing a situation which had existed for some time when they induced Docemo to cede Lagos as a colony, thus establishing the first British territorial annexation in Nigeria.

At the same time, a similar creeping and almost unnoticed extension of British control was occurring in the Fante areas of the Gold Coast. Here the vital British problem was revenue, for although legitimate trade did expand, there was no commodity comparable to Nigerian palm oil. Much of the difficulty was due to the presence of the Danish and Dutch forts, for it was impossible to raise customs duties when Africans would merely evade them by taking their goods to the Dutch or Danish outlets. In 1850 the Gold Coast was made independent of Sierra Leone and given a governor of its own, and at the same time the Danish forts were purchased by Britain. It was hoped that the Dutch would also sell, but the negotiations for this failed. In 1852, therefore, the British began an interesting experiment in "parliamentary" government. At a meeting of all the coastal rulers which was constituted into a "Legislative Assembly," the chiefs agreed to raise sums for road-building, schools, and hospitals by levying a poll tax on their people. The project, however, was a dismal failure. The chiefs were attempting to arrogate to themselves a power which they did not possess in traditional political theory; there was widespread resistance and rioting against the taxes, and the amount actually collected proved so small that the scheme had to be abandoned. This first popular resistance to British policies, and the way in which the British backed down, were to prove important precedents.

Meanwhile relations with Ashanti, which had been reasonably stable since 1831, began to deteriorate. The growth of British influence began to alarm the Ashanti, especially as the result increasingly strengthened the Fante, who were beginning to produce skilled and educated minorities as a result of the impact of the Basel Mission, which arrived in the 1820s, and of the Wesleyans arriving in the 1830s. Though the Ashanti could still obtain firearms through the Dutch in Elmina, there was now nowhere on the Gold Coast from which they could export slaves. In 1863 the Ashanti demanded that the British governor surrender some refugees from Kumasi, and Governor Pine refused. The Ashanti armies now swept down to the coast. Governor Pine wished to meet them with strong forces, but the British government was so alarmed by the prospect of extending its activities that he was forbidden to counterattack.

The Ashanti invasion provoked a fundamental re-assessment of British policy, bringing into the open growing fears in Parliament at the extension of British political interference. Besides the theoretical objections of the free traders, and the obvious contrast between the prosperous and independent Oil Rivers and the poor and dependent Gold Coast, those in Britain who were interested in colonial expansion felt that energies were better directed to colonies in Australia and New Zealand than to the "white man's grave" of West Africa. In 1865 a Select Committee of Parliament investigated the state of the British West African Settlements and concluded that the trend of policy must be reversed. Though it agreed that Sierra Leone must remain a permanent British settlement, the committee declared that the other settlements must be abandoned. Where this was impossible at once, steps should be taken to prepare Africans for the transition to self-government.

The policy thus announced was in fact unrealistic. It ignored the extent to which missionaries, traders, and liberated Africans had already involved Britain in the politics of the Gold Coast and Nigeria, and it failed to take account of the ambitions of British representatives on the spot, who were not willingly going to carry out policies which would deprive them of their careers. It naturally alarmed the Fante, who had already been disconcerted by Britain's failure to stand up to the Ashanti invasion of 1863. It has been seen that the origins of the Fante Confederation lay in their common fear of Ashanti. Now their fear of being abandoned by the British provoked a most interesting movement, in which may be seen the origins of Gold Coast nationalism. There was by now a sizable minority of educated Africans among the Fante, some native to the Gold Coast, a few of Sierra Leone origin. All of these men were mission-trained and Christian, and the more enterprising among them had already achieved posts of some eminence. They had begun newspapers in Cape Coast; many were clergymen, others were qualified to practice as lawyers, and a handful had entered the British colonial service as administrative officers. One James Bannerman had even served as acting governor for a time. This nucleus of an educated élite now seized on the fears of the traditional Fante chiefs to propose the establishment of a new nation, whose objects would be progressive and reformist. For the chiefs the goal was to build up Fante unity and military power to resist the Ashanti; for the intellectuals it was this also, but much more.

Against a background of constant tension with Ashanti and fears of British withdrawal, the Fante chiefs began a series of meetings at Mankessim. In October 1871 they finally agreed on a written constitution to "promote and advance the political and constitutional position of our peoples." A Fante Confederation was established, with a king-president elected from the kings of the independent states. A parliament was set up, in which each king would sit together with one educated man for each state. The parliament could pass laws and levy taxes. Local assessors, who would be educated Africans, would control local administration, and their duties, set down in detail, included road-building, establishment of schools, agricultural education, and the improvement of drainage. The constitution was a remarkable attempt to blend the old and the new, to harmonize the desires of the old aristocracy and the new élite. It was in no sense anti-British, for its authors saw it as part of the policy of the 1865 committee, and asked for all the help they could get from Britain to ensure the success of the new nation.

They failed to understand, however, the reaction of the local British officials. The acting governor, to whom the papers were presented, immediately lost his temper, regarded the whole movement as subversive, and arrested the delegates who had brought the constitution to him. Though the Colonial Office condemned this hasty action and ordered the release of the arrested men, the damage had been done, and the Mankessim movement petered out.

In fact, the development of British influence was moving in the opposite direction, despite the policy laid down in 1865. In 1869, in order to improve revenue, the British had finally succeeded in purchasing the Dutch forts. This meant that at last there was a hope of the Gold Coast paying its way. The British had some doubts regarding the Dutch headquarters of Elmina, for the Dutch paid rent for it to Ashanti. In 1871, however, they secured a document from the *asantehene* in which he supposedly renounced all title to Elmina. In reality the document was a forgery, which the Ashanti regarded as a *causa belli*, and in January 1873 the main Ashanti armies crossed the Pra, determined to deal with the British once and for all.

For the first time the British responded by meeting the Ashanti challenge head on. The Ashanti were delayed by early rains, and the time was used to bring out 2,500 regular British troops under General Sir Garnet Wolseley, and to amass thousands of Fante allies. In 1874 the combined armies led by Wolseley advanced into Ashanti, smashed the Ashanti armies, and occupied Kumasi. The Ashanti submitted to dictated peace terms, agreed to pay 50,000 ounces of gold, to abolish human sacrifice, to open the road to Kumasi to trade, and to renounce all claims to the coastal states. Wolseley's troops then withdrew.

Having destroyed the Fante Confederation, and having accepted responsibility for dealing with the Ashanti menace, the British had virtually taken control of the affairs of the southern Gold Coast, despite the decision to withdraw in 1865. The purchase of the Dutch forts placed the whole coastline firmly under British control. In July 1874 these developments were openly accepted when the British Government declared the area south of, but not including, Ashanti a British colony. This declaration was unilateral—there was no attempt to create colonial rule by renegotiating and strengthening the bonds of 1844—and as such it was resented by the rulers and educated elements who had attempted to build a new nation through the Mankessim constitution. But there was little that they could do about it.

In Nigeria there was much more of an effort to implement the spirit of the 1865 report. Although there was no attempt at withdrawal, the government did restrict ambitious local officials in their attempts to extend British authority. In the Oil Rivers, although consular influence undoubtedly increased, and many of the states established "Courts of Equity" in which the voice of British traders was predominant and which sometimes called on the consul to enforce their decisions, and although there was much interference in the politics of Bonny, the policy stopped short of open control. In 1879 petitions from Christian groups in the Cameroons asking for British rule east of the Oil Rivers were rejected, despite support from the consul, who would have liked to establish his headquarters in this cool and healthy mountain area. On the Niger River there was a similar tendency to reduce British commitments after 1865. With the development of a regular trade after 1854, the coastal middlemen, especially those of Brass, began to resist by force this penetration of their palm oil markets, and they were encouraged and armed by their Liverpool allies. The Foreign Office had thus seen fit to provide naval escorts for the Niger traders in the 1860s, and in 1866 a consul was appointed at Lokoja. In 1869, however, the consulate was withdrawn, and two years later the British negotiated an agreement with *emir* Masaba of Nupe, whereby he agreed to protect

British traders on the Niger in return for arms supplies, and the naval protection was withdrawn.

In Lagos, annexed in 1861 as a British colony, it seemed at first that the British would inevitably expand along the coast and into the interior. British colonies were expected to balance their expenditure with local revenues, but it was impossible to levy sufficient money in Lagos if merchants could avoid high duties by moving a few miles along the coast to Porto Novo. Moreover, the Yoruba civil wars seriously disrupted regular trade, and it was in the interest of local governors of Lagos to try to intervene in Yorubaland to increase and stabilize the flow of trade. Governor Glover of Lagos had extensive ambitions, believing that a profitable chain of commerce could be built from Lagos to Ibadan, and from there through Ilorin to the Muslim north and Nupe. Ibadan, the largest urban center in the south, became the key to his strategy, but the Egba state of Abeokuta could not sit idly by and allow Ibadan to build a direct link with Lagos and secure unlimited arms. The Egba, therefore, pushed across Ibadan's route to Lagos, until Glover dislodged them by force in March 1865. Relations with Abeokuta, once the darling of the British, now came close to war. The educated Egba formed the Egba United Board of Management, designed to modernize the state and set up regular customs posts along the border with Lagos. Glover moved troops up to the border, and the Egba responded by expelling all white missionaries from Abeokuta in 1867. Glover was increasingly active in the interior; in 1871 he summoned a conference of all the important Yoruba states in an attempt to end the civil wars, but failed. He then tried to blockade Porto Novo in order to cut off the supply of arms to the Egba, and began considering stopping all trade with Yorubaland. This action alienated the British merchants and, as he had already been rebuked by the Colonial Office for interference in areas outside his jurisdiction, he was therefore recalled. Subsequent governors were kept more firmly to the official British policy of non-interference.

In general, the British held firm in their reluctance to expand territory and indulge in colonial adventures. This reluctance was based on fears of incurring responsibility and expenditure, dislike of posting colonial officials to an unhealthy area, and above all on the belief that while the real British interests at stake (i.e., the expansion of British trade and missionary endeavor) prospered, there was no case for colonial rule. On the whole, this view was amply justified in the period from 1807 to 1880. Most of the African states involved showed themselves to be sufficiently well organized to provide the necessary protection for both commerce and missionaries, and even in war-torn Yorubaland not a single British trader or missionary lost his life by violence. The annexation of Lagos in 1861 and the declaration of the Gold Coast Colony in 1874 were exceptions to the general trend. Lagos was annexed initially to provide a secure anti-slave trade port for Abeokuta, and the Gold Coast Colony was an attempt to stem the tide of Ashanti advance. Both colonies were kept close, with their hinterlands left under independent African rule.

The Establishment of British Rule

The attitudes just described rested on a basic condition which was often lost sight of before 1880—the condition that the British should be allowed to pursue their policies of "Christianity and Commerce" without interference from other European powers. Because of their early start in the industrial revolution, the British could defeat simple trade competition from French and German firms, and they were not unduly worried at the activities of foreign missionaries in areas of predominant British influence. Thus the Basel Mission had become the chief missionary agency in the Gold Coast, and French Catholic missionaries established themselves at Onitsha on the Niger. The prospect of foreign colonies, however, was a more serious matter, for colonies (especially those of France) usually meant the establishment of protective tariffs to shut out British traders.

Before 1880, however, there was little threat of foreign colonial activity in or around either the Gold Coast or the Niger. Europe was periodically convulsed by the crises and revolutions unleased by liberalism, nationalism, and radical democracy. Germany and Italy were not united nation-states until 1870, and the French changed their constitutional regime in 1830, 1848, 1852, and 1870. From time to time the French pursued colonial ventures, especially under Napoleon III (1852-70), but much of their attention was directed to the subjugation of Algeria, where the French conquest began in 1830 and military campaigns continued throughout the century.

After 1870, however, a new pattern began to emerge in Europe. Germany and Italy became nation-states, and Bismarck, the German chancellor, began to build an alliance system that prevented France from mounting a war of revenge for her crushing defeat and the loss of Alsace and Lorraine to Germany in 1870. France and Italy both began to turn to Africa as a field for expansion, and especially as a market for their infant industries which needed protection against British and German competition. Bismarck encouraged these ambitions—especially those of France—which he thought would divert French energies from European affairs. At the same time, he rightly believed that French colonial activity in Africa would alarm the British and drive Britain and France apart diplomatically, for the only real threat to Germany lay in the possibility of an Anglo-French alliance.

In 1879 the French, having deposed the monarchist President Macmahon, at last established the Third Republic on a firm footing. This resulted almost immediately in expansionist activity in West Africa, with French expeditions pushing out from Senegal into the savannah areas around the Niger sources. There was little in this to alarm the British, for these were regions remote from areas of British commercial predominance. Much more alarming was the development of French activity in and around the lower Niger after 1880. In 1880 two French firms began trading on the Niger. The chief agent of one of them was appointed consular agent with powers to make treaties on behalf of France, and unsuccessful French attempts were made to secure a protectorate over Brass which was foiled only at the last minute by the influence of Bishop Crowther's African clergy. The French competition was a direct threat to the United African Company, formed by George Goldie Taubman (later Sir George Goldie) in 1879 by amalgamating all the competing British firms on the Niger to secure a monopoly. Goldie now began considering ways to meet the French threat by securing political and administrative powers for his company, and in 1882 he reformed it as the National African Company, with articles of association allowing the company to accept new political and administrative powers. Goldie now embarked on a price war designed to bankrupt the French traders.

There were other alarming signs of French activity. In 1882 the

French reasserted their claim to Porto Novo, and began preparations to occupy the port effectively. The move not only had serious implications for Lagos, Porto Novo's rival, but also threatened to involve the French in Yorubaland. The British consul in the Oil Rivers also began sending alarming reports; between 1879 and 1882 the French had established a new colony of Gabun south of the Cameroons, and the British consul feared that they might penetrate from there behind the city-states of the Oil Rivers to tap the palm oil trade directly in the Ibo hinterland. He urged that Britain should annex the Cameroons to block this advance.

The British government responded to these pressures slowly and cautiously. British trade on the Niger and Oil Rivers was large, and warranted some measure of protection, but the Colonial Office refused to establish a colonial regime. The Foreign Office then agreed to establish over the Oil Rivers and the Cameroons a "protectorate" administered by the consul, in which the kings of the city-states would surrender their power to have independent relations with other states, and thus prevent a French take-over; but even this minimal action, decided in 1882, was delayed for nearly two years in face of the refusal of the Treasury to find £5,000 for "presents" with which to sweeten the African rulers. In the meantime, Bismarck had decided on direct German intervention designed to convince the British of their dependence on Germany, and when the British consul arrived at last in the Cameroons in 1884 he found himself forestalled, and the German flag flying. He hurriedly completed his treaties in the Oil Rivers, which was then declared a British protectorate.

It was soon evident that the German intervention was to mean more than the loss of the Cameroons, for Germany had also annexed Togoland, which, with the French claim to Porto Novo, now prevented any possibility of joining the British Gold Coast with the Colony of Nigeria, and in effect determining that Ghana and Nigeria should henceforth develop as separate countries. Moreover, France and Germany now began to cooperate with each other against Britain in Africa, and at the end of 1884 summoned a Conference in Berlin to discuss the future of the Congo and Niger rivers, both regions of British commercial predominance.

The Berlin Conference of 1884-85 effectively destroyed British influence on the Congo, but the British position was saved on the Niger, largely as a result of the efforts of Goldie. Before the conference met he was able to announce that his trade war had bankrupted the French firms and that they had sold out to him. At this point Franco-German cooperation began to break down, and after the Conference had drawn up a Niger Navigation Act establishing "free navigation" on the river, Britain was declared to be the power responsible for enforcing the act on the lower Niger. Goldie now demanded that the British government grant his company a royal charter to administer the Niger, and as this arrangement promised to secure British control without expense to the taxpayer, it was finally adopted in 1886, whereupon Goldie renamed his company the Royal Niger Company.

The "scramble" of 1884-85 thus resulted in the political separation of the Gold Coast from Nigeria, and left the British in control of the coastlines of both countries. It had little immediate effect, however, on the African peoples concerned, most of whom had no idea of the significance of what had taken place. On the Gold Coast there was no move to expand into the interior or to take over Ashanti, and in Nigeria the new protectorate of the Oil Rivers, theoretically carrying British control from east of the Lagos colony to Calabar, was at first little different from the "consul and gunboat" influence which preceded it. On the Niger it might seem that the Royal Niger Company was inaugurating a new and aggressively imperialistic spirit, for it began, immediately on receipt of its charter, to make vast territorial claims based on treaties made since 1884. By virtue of documents brought back from Sokoto and Gwandu the company claimed complete overlordship of the Fulani empire, and through hundreds of treaties made with the Igala, Ibo, and Ijo of the lower Niger it claimed territorial dominion down to the sea. Most of these documents were spurious, however, and the company had no intention of provoking a war with the Fulani by trying to establish actual authority in the north. Even along the river banks it was more concerned with creating a monopoly against rival British and African traders by vexatious licenses and customs duties, than it was with ruling the territory. In this the Niger company was eminently successful: its rivals were gradually squeezed out, its dividends steadied at 6 per cent, and by 1893 it was the sole trading organization on the river.

The Oil Rivers was left outside the Niger Company's rule, for the Liverpool traders to the city-states were vehement opponents of the Niger trade which cut behind their middlemen. Nevertheless, the lesson of interior penetration was not lost on them, and they began to use the new consular protectorate as a means of breaking their dependence on the middlemen. The treaties with the city-states of 1884 had contained a clause granting "free trade," but King Ja Ja of Opobo had insisted on striking out this clause in the treaty which he had signed. Ja Ja was originally a slave, brought to Bonny, where he had prospered and become the head of the richest "house." He had become so powerful by the 1860s that his rivals had tried to strike him down, but he had cleverly abandoned Bonny and founded the new state of Opobo with himself as king (thus becoming the first ex-slave to achieve this status) in 1869. Opobo captured many of Bonny's interior palm oil markets and soon became the center of the oil trade. Ja Ja concluded monopolistic arrangements with Miller Brothers, a Glasgow firm which had supported him in 1869 so as to break into the Liverpool dominated markets, and the Liverpool firms reacted by plotting the downfall of Ja Ja. When the protectorate treaty with Opobo was signed, Ja Ja had been astute enough to demand a definition from the consul as to the precise meaning of the word "protection," and had been informed in writing that it meant that the Queen wished to protect him from foreign aggression but would not interfere in his internal affairs. It was probably meant sincerely—in 1884. By 1887, however, Liverpool traders were ascending rivers claimed by Ja Ja as his, and trading directly in markets which he claimed, and Ja Ja retaliated by "making ju ju" (i.e., by forcing the people to swear binding oaths) and stopping trade. The acting consul, Harry Johnston, under pressure from the Liverpool firms, inveigled Ja Ja to a meeting on board a British warship under promise of safe conduct, and deported him to the Gold Coast, where he was later exiled to the West Indies. Though Ja Ja was allowed to return from exile a few years later, the decision came too late, for he died before he could reach Opobo. His tragic, and for the British none too creditable, story has made him a national martyr in Nigeria.

Ja Ja's deportation, however, was not yet typical of an aggressive British imperialism. Until 1892 the British were bent on holding their control with as little expense and responsibility as possible. The reason for this pause was that the French before 1892 were in no position to threaten the British. They were advancing overland from Senegal into the savannah zone, but were as yet a long way from the rear of the Gold Coast, let alone the Niger Company's sphere of influence. Much more dangerous was their position on the coast of Dahomey, where they had established themselves in Porto Novo and Cotonou, but here they were blocked from entry into Yorubaland by the kings of Dahomey. In 1888 the British governor of Lagos induced the *alafin* of Oyo to sign a treaty placing his dominions under British protection, but this paper claim was more for French than African consumption, and resulted in no actual British administration.

In 1892 the French declared war on Dahomey, and by 1893 had taken Abomey, the capital, and deposed the king. It was soon apparent that the French were bent on more than the assertion of paper control. French officials were stationed in each Dahomeyan town, with small garrisons of trained African soldiers under white officers. The French now began to elaborate a doctrine of "effective occupation," arguing that they could not recognize British claims where there was no evidence of a real occupation by white British officials, or no troops under white officers. In 1894 they pushed rapidly north of Dahomey into Borgu, which lay immediately north of Yorubaland and west of the Niger Company's sphere, and began occupying Borguan towns in force, even though Goldie had succeeded, through Frederick Lugard whom the Niger Company employed for this purpose, in obtaining treaties with the Borguan towns only a few days before the French arrived.

It was the French advance into Dahomey which prompted the British to act in Yorubaland. Since 1886 the British had become virtually the predominant power in Yorubaland, for in that year the governor of Lagos had succeeded in persuading delegates from all the Yoruba states (except Ilorin) to settle terms of peace. But thereafter war constantly threatened to erupt once more, especially as both Ijebu and Abeokuta, though bitterly hostile to each other, equally feared the consequences of allowing open trade between

Lagos and Ibadan. Of the two states, Ijebu was least adept at dealing with the British, for she had rejected Christian missions, expelled her own Christian and literate citizens, and thus deprived herself of skilled negotiators and advisors. In fact, exiled Ijebu living in Lagos worked for British control so as to overthrow what they regarded as a cruel and obscurantist regime. After a series of incidents involving the manhandling of British officials visiting Ijebu, the king of Ijebu went so far as to demand from Ibadan the heads of two CMS missionaries in Ibadan, one of whom was an Ijebu exile, on the charge that they had illegally smuggled arms to Ibadan through Ijebu territory. Carter, the governor of Lagos, sensing the threat of the French in Dahomey, decided to attack and subdue Ijebu, hoping for a chain reaction in the rest of Yorubaland. In May 1892 British forces marched into Ijebu. In 1893 Carter followed this up with a grand tour through Yorubaland, where he made treaties with Abeokuta and Oyo granting the British overall judicial powers, entrenching toleration for missionaries and Christians, and agreeing to keep roads open. Ibadan at first refused to sign, but finally accepted a treaty in August 1893. The 1893 treaties began a rapid process by which the British extended the authority of the Lagos colony to cover all Yorubaland, so that by 1896 only Ilorin remained independent. Except for the Ijebu war, and a minor military expedition to coerce the *alafin* of Oyo in 1895, the establishment of British rule in Yorubaland had been accomplished without bloodshed. Several factors contributed to this: the Yoruba themselves were exhausted by their internecine wars and to some extent cowed by the rapid defeat of Ijebu, and the Christian Yoruba actively worked to secure treaties with the British and the establishment of a *pax Britannica*.

The presence of French forces in Borgu, from whence they could move into northern Nigeria, remained as a threat to British interests. This threat was complicated by the fact that Ilorin remained outside Lagos control. As a Muslim state allied with Nupe and the Fulani, Ilorin continued to harry Ibadan and refused to submit to the general *pax*. The Lagos regime would have loved to subdue Ilorin, but Goldie claimed that Ilorin was within the Niger Company's sphere of influence. Joseph Chamberlain, who had become colonial secretary in 1895, forbade Lagos to act, but told

Goldie that he must himself conquer Ilorin. In 1897 Goldie personally led the company's troops first against Nupe, whose *emir* was deposed, and then against Ilorin, where the *emir* was made to sign a treaty of submission.

These military campaigns were the beginning of the end for Goldie's chartered company. The company was already under attack in the press and parliament for its ruthless monopolistic practices, and in 1895 the city-state of Brass had actually invaded and sacked the company's headquarters at Akassa. A Commission of Inquiry into the affair revealed that the Brass attack had been provoked by the way in which the company had forcibly excluded them from the Niger trade. The Ilorin and Nupe campaigns now created a situation which the company could not face alone and unaided. For the first time British forces had attacked Fulani *emirs*, and Sokoto and Gwandu, incensed at this affront, prepared to unleash their forces on the company, if only they could secure unity in their disunited dominions. The French took advantage of the campaign in Ilorin to move troops and French officers into Bussa, from whence the Niger was navigable down to the sea. The company could not even hope for assistance from the south, for in 1897 British forces were occupied in the subjugation of Benin in retaliation for the ambushing of a party of officials and troops of the Niger Coast Protectorate (as the Oil Rivers Protectorate was renamed in 1893).

In 1897, in order to defend the Company's frontiers, Chamberlain appointed Frederick Lugard to command what was to become the West African Frontier Force, and to reply to French encroachments with similar "effective occupation." In this way the British taxpayer began to foot the bill for control of northern Nigeria, and the Niger Company lost its *raison d'être*. Its death was slow, for Chamberlain hesitated to get rid of the company until the crisis of Anglo-French rivalry in Borgu had come to an end. In 1898 France and Britain signed an agreement which virtually fixed the northern and western frontiers of Nigeria. (The eastern frontiers had been settled by an Anglo-German agreement of 1893.) There followed some months of bargaining with Goldie before the Niger Company was bought out, with handsome compensation. Finally, on January 1, 1900, the company's flag was hauled down and Lugard assumed control as high commissioner of the new Protectorate of Northern Nigeria.

The British now had an internationally recognized claim to the area within the frontiers of modern Nigeria, and were, in fact, in effective control of Yorubaland, Benin, and the coastal city-states of the Niger delta and Oil Rivers. Vast areas of the east and north, however, had still to be subdued. Moreover, these were all areas with practically no history of close contact with the British, and no understanding of or sympathy with British purposes. Both the Fulani and the Ibo had long traditions of independence and could be subdued only by force. From 1900 Lugard organized a series of campaigns against the Fulani *emirs*, and by 1906 all resistance had been crushed. In Bornu the ruler was brought under control without force by the offer to protect him against French demands. Among the Ibo and Ibibio the task of establishing control was even more difficult than in the north. In 1902 British forces attacked Aro-Chuku and Chuku's cave was destroyed and its roof blown off. It was hoped that destruction of the Aro would result in an easy occupation of Ibo country, but instead the British often had to fight for each village. The years from 1900 until as late as 1911 saw a steady military advance into Ibo areas both from the south and from the river cities such as Onitsha.

In the Gold Coast the pattern of British advance was similarly conditioned by French, and to some extent by German, activities. The German annexation of Togoland in 1884 and the German advances to secure a viable coastline and push inland provoked British moves to annex Akwamu, Krepi, and the Ga and Ewe areas in order to try to control the Volta River mouth. This had the effect of splitting the Ewe people between British and German administration.

Though the French occupied territory west of the Gold Coast which was constituted into the separate Ivory Coast colony in 1893, the French had little interest in the Gold Coast hinterland before 1894, being more concerned to link the Ivory Coast with their activities in the savannah area. The British were thus able to conduct their affairs here in a much more leisurely fashion than in Nigeria. They showed little inclination to swallow up Ashanti, which was seriously weakened by the defeat of 1874. In the aftermath of their defeat the Ashanti destooled the *asantehene* and replaced him with Mensa Bonsu (1874-83), who cautiously began to rebuild the shat-

tered empire, but was careful not to alarm either the British or the
Fante by activity too near the colony area. His somewhat ignoble intrigues provoked opposition from the younger and wilder spirits, in
whose view he was humiliating the nation by his constant accession to
British views. In February 1883 Mensa Bonsu was destooled, and
five years of anarchy and intermittent civil war between various
claimants to the throne followed. The Ashanti chiefs even requested
a British representative to assist them in sorting out the tangle of the
succession, which could have provided an opportunity for Britain
to begin to control Ashanti, had she wished to do so, but no attempt
at control was made until 1888, when British mediation secured the
installment of Prempeh, a youth of sixteen. As soon as the British
mediators left, civil war erupted once more.

The British now began to become alarmed at the possibility of
French or German intervention, for the Germans were pushing
north from Togoland, while in 1888 the French from the Ivory
Coast had secured a treaty with Gyaman, once part of the Ashanti
empire. The British, therefore, began to offer protectorate treaties to
states within the Ashanti empire seeking to escape control of the
Ashanti, thus further adding to Prempeh's difficulties. But Prempeh
began to show remarkable ability as he grew up, and by 1890 he was
within sight of restoring Ashanti to something like its former
glories. When the British sent an impressive delegation to Kumasi
in December 1890, with a draft treaty of protection, Prempeh rejected it after careful consideration. For the next three years he
intensified his efforts to reconquer the disaffected states on the
frontiers, with considerable success.

The British had withheld their intervention until it was too late,
and, as the French now began moving into Mossi and the savannah
states north of Ashanti, the threat became serious. The British tried
to respond by sending one of their ablest officials, George Ekem
Ferguson, a brilliant explorer, a qualified surveyor, and the first
African to become a Fellow of the Royal Geographical Society.
Ferguson succeeded between 1892 and 1894 in making treaties with
most of the important states of the north, including Dagomba,
Dagarti, Mamprussi, and Mossi, but the French refused to recognize
treaties made by an African, and again asserted their doctrine of
effective occupation. For the British it was impossible to occupy

these areas in strength while Ashanti lay across the routes to the colony area.

In 1893, therefore, the British demanded that the *asantehene* accept a British resident in Kumasi and promise to abandon warfare as an instrument for reuniting the Ashanti empire. In return he and his chiefs would receive regular stipends from the British. The Ashanti were tempted by this offer, yet rightly distrustful, and at the same time they were afraid to provoke a British invasion. They therefore embarked upon a most novel and interesting scheme. A poll tax of ten shillings a head was raised in order to finance an embassy in London, which would have the effect of asserting Ashanti independence without offending Britain, and at the same time would provide a means of bypassing the Gold Coast governor, whom they distrusted. The embassy in fact set sail in March 1895, despite attempts by the governor to stop it.

This move was too late, for the British had already decided to conquer Ashanti by force. The *asantehene* was given an ultimatum that he must receive a British resident, and his reply—that he would await the result of his embassy's negotiations—was brushed aside. Over 2,000 regular troops were assembled, and in January 1896 they invaded Ashanti. The Ashanti did not resist, and Kumasi was occupied without fighting; Prempeh had decided to avoid bloodshed and submit to "the white man's rule." The governor now demanded Prempeh's complete submission and an indemnity of 50,000 ounces of gold. Prempeh submitted at once, embracing the governor's feet, but declared that he could not possibly pay so large a sum. The governor thereupon arrested Prempeh, the queen-mother, and four other members of the royalty, as well as five *omanhenes*, and took them as prisoners to the coast.

For their king to be treated in such a way was degrading and humiliating to the Ashanti, but worse was to follow. The British proceeded to break up the Ashanti confederacy by making separate treaties with each of the states composing it, while Kumasi remained with no ruler at all. Ashanti resentment naturally grew, with the final spark to the embers of revolt coming in 1900, when the British governor demanded to sit on the golden stool, which the British had never succeeded in capturing. This demand was a terrible blasphemy to the Ashanti, for not even the *asantehene* was allowed to actually sit on the sacred stool. Revolt flared up immediately, and took a year to suppress. As a result, Ashanti was formally annexed as a colony in 1901. The occupation of Ashanti in 1896 allowed the British to push north along the Ashanti trade routes and to establish themselves in the savannah states, which were constituted as the Northern Territories and given protectorate status.

Thus, by 1901, British control had been established within the frontiers of the modern states of Ghana and Nigeria. The process had been somewhat haphazard, beginning with the "exceptional" annexation of Lagos in 1861 and the creation of the Gold Coast Colony in 1874. The French and German pressures of the 1880s had led the British to secure control of the coastlines, but with little enthusiasm for direct colonial administration. In the early 1890s this pressure had pushed the British into the hinterlands, and by 1895, with the colonial secretaryship of Joseph Chamberlain, a definite imperialist spirit had entered British activity, leading to the conquest of Ashanti, the formation of the West African Frontier Force, and the conquest of northern Nigeria. As yet neither Nigeria nor the Gold Coast formed single administrative units. The Gold Coast consisted of the colony area in the south, Ashanti, which was a colony but a separate unit under the Gold Coast governor, and the Protectorate of the Northern Territories. Nigeria consisted of three separate units of government under three different governors. The north became the Protectorate of Northern Nigeria with Lugard as High Commissioner in 1900; the Oil Rivers area and its Ibo hinterland was taken over by the Colonial Office as the Protectorate of Southern Nigeria, while Lagos and its Yoruba-protected states remained under the governor of Lagos.

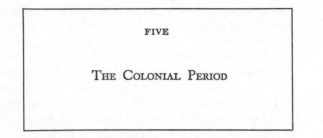

FIVE

THE COLONIAL PERIOD

Colonial Rule and Economic Life

The predominant purposes of British activity in the nineteenth century had been to transform the African societies of Ghana and Nigeria into free trading communities producing tropical raw materials and consuming British manufactures. British rule had been established to protect these economic interests. The new British colonies thus began with an already developed trading basis. At first the British administrations had little in the way of a positive policy of economic development. British liberal economic theory did not accept the idea that the state had any role in organizing production or in accumulating and investing capital, except in roads and harbors, and in colonial affairs it was axiomatic that a colony must live from its own resources, without subsidies from the metropolitan power. What the state refused, private British capitalists were no more willing to provide. The British economic interests in West Africa were dominated by traders and shippers, already making steady profits simply transporting and marketing African produce, and they showed no inclination to take risks by investing capital in new methods of production or in industrial development, with the sole exception of mining.

Despite this lack of any planned or purposeful action for economic development, the effects of the establishment of British rule upon the economies of Nigeria and Ghana were profound. The destruction of the independence of the African states which comprised the new colonies created free markets of a size hitherto unprecedented. Internal tolls on the movement of goods disappeared, and movement of persons became easy and safe. The suppression of internal slave trading and raiding forced the profit motive to concentrate on productive occupations, and the spread of a uniform *pax* created a security of person and property which intensified the accumulation of goods, savings, and capital.

Moreover, British administration itself had direct economic effects. The number of white officials grew steadily, especially after Ross's discovery in 1897 that malaria was transmitted by the mosquito, which led to the widespread use of netting and the draining of stagnant pools where mosquitoes could breed. The employment of African clerks also increased, and Africans earned wages in the police and army on an increasing scale. These activities centered around the administrative stations and attracted unofficial wage-earners such as gardeners, servants, tailors, watchmen, launderers, and the like. Much larger groups congregated in the colonial or regional capitals like Lagos, Accra, Kumasi, or Calabar, where the needs of the administration developed crafts—most of which had already been established by the missions—such as printing, carpentry, construction work, mechanical repairs, and market gardening, as well as service employments. In all these centers where steadily growing groups of wage-earners developed, the retail trade expanded, nearby farmers began bringing food to market, rents began to be charged, and barter disappeared to be replaced with currency transactions.

These administrative centers (which, of course, were often located in traditional urban centers) naturally became junctions in the network of roads, for the administrators built roads as much for their own convenience and for rapid movement of police and troops as for commercial motives. Many of the early British district officers were fanatical road builders, for without development funds, and practically without cash revenues in the early days, road construction was one of the few tangible things they could achieve. (There is an excellent portrayal of such a character in Joyce Cary's novel of Nigeria, *Mr. Johnson.*) In traditional society able bodied males had the obligation to maintain roads, and the British officials could call on this source of manpower to build unsurfaced earth roads and simple bridges using nearby timber. In this way the administrative centers tended to become collecting centers for local produce, where African middlemen brought goods for sale to European buyers and took away European imports for distribution. They also tended to attract the mission schools, especially those which tried to impart higher education in English to senior pupils, and which needed to draw on a wide area.

The towns thus came to be centers of economic opportunity, of political influence, and of education, and they naturally attracted ambitious Africans, especially able men who had little status according to traditional social values. Africans in the towns became enmeshed in cash relationships, and were stimulated to new wants, such as the bicycle, which became a symbol of achievement. In the towns tribe mixed with tribe, and custom was watered down, and these new wants and attitudes filtered back from the towns to the more conservative rural areas.

Thus, the mere imposition of British rule and the growth of cash-oriented African minorities were sufficient to produce a steady rise in the trade of the Gold Coast, Lagos, and Southern Nigeria from 1880 to 1895, without any major British capital investments. The rise in trade meant increasing yields from customs duties, and by the early 1890s the colonial governors were considering methods of investing surpluses to produce further economic advances. It was not difficult to conclude that the chief impediment to further development was the lack of an effective transport system. Only on the Niger, in the Oil Rivers area, and to a lesser extent on the Volta River was the shipment of goods relatively simple, with the steamers fed by networks of canoe transport. Once away from river access, transport over long distances by human porterage became prohibitively expensive (except for gold dust), and this cost increased with the gradual eradication of slavery. Moreover, it was known that mineral deposits existed—gold in the Gold Coast, tin in Northern Nigeria—but extensive deep mining operations were impossible when the necessary heavy machinery could not be placed on the spot. Railways were clearly the obvious answer to these problems.

In the 1880s various private British syndicates had asked for concessions to build railways in the Gold Coast and from Lagos into Yorubaland, but all required some sort of British guarantee of interest on their capital. In 1885 the Colonial Office announced that if it were satisfied that a railway would pay, then the colonial government itself would construct and operate the line. The government firmly held to this policy in the subsequent years, and the railways thus became state enterprises when they were constructed. After 1891 the serious work of surveying prospective lines in the Gold Coast and from Lagos was started. In 1896 construction began at Lagos of the line which reached Ibadan in 1900, and then slowly crept up into northern Nigeria, where the northern governor had created a separate system which was joined to the Lagos line in 1911. Construction of a railway system for eastern Nigeria did not begin until 1913, when the line was begun from the newly constructed Port Harcourt to Enugu, the new regional capital which was to replace Calabar. Enugu was reached in 1916, and between 1919 and 1931 the eastern line was extended across the Benue River to join the northern system.

There was no attempt to build such long lines of rail in the Gold Coast, and the Northern Territories were left without railways. The railways were begun essentially to make extensive gold mining operations possible, and thus the first line, begun at Sekondi in 1898, ran through the gold bearing districts up to Kumasi, which it reached in 1903. The rapid growth of the cocoa industry created demands for a line further east, and in 1923 a line from Accra to Kumasi was completed. The two Gold Coast lines were then linked by the Huni valley line, finished in 1927. The forest zone of the Gold Coast was thus more intensively covered by rail than any other area of tropical Africa.

The railways had dramatic results, especially on mining activity. In 1901 the Gold Coast exported only £22,000 worth of gold; by 1903 when the rails reached Kumasi this had risen to £255,000; by 1907 gold exports were worth over £1 million and by 1913 over £1.5 million. Ancillary mining also developed on a lesser scale for diamonds and manganese. In Nigeria the tin mining industry showed much the same development, and the value of tin exports from the plateau area rose from £25,000 in 1907 to £708,000 in 1914.

The mining companies were entirely European owned, for only European companies were able to amass sufficient capital to acquire expensive mining machinery, and isolated efforts to do so by educated Gold Coast Africans failed. European capital also secured control of banking with the establishment in the 1890s of the Bank

of British West Africa controlled by A. L. Jones, the shipping mag-
nate of Liverpool who already controlled the Elder Dempster shipping lines to West Africa. The new bank, operating in all the
British West African colonies, soon obtained the privilege of currency issue and acted as banker to the colonial governments. In
its credit operations it adopted normal conservative British standards of security for loans, so that it was of little value to Africans
in extending their range of economic investment.

Wholesale trade and the bulk import-export trade also fell under
virtually complete non-African control; in this field the nineteenth-
century efforts of king Ja Ja and a few other African merchants
to ship direct to England had been none too successful. At the
end of the nineteenth century there were already signs of increasing monopolistic tendencies among the European traders, exempli-
fied by the Royal Niger Company. After 1888 there were negotiations for amalgamation of the Niger Company with all the traders
of Liverpool and Glasgow, but these fell through, partly as a result
of King Ja Ja's deposition, which was bitterly resented by the Glasgow firm of Miller Brothers who were agents for Ja Ja. The Liverpool
traders came together, however, as the African Association Limited,
and in 1892 the Association and the Niger Company began inter-
locking directors on each other's boards. The real pressure toward
monopoly, however, came with the rise of the giant firm of Lever
Brothers. William Lever, a self-made businessman, had built up a
large soap manufacturing concern in Cheshire by the early twentieth
century, partly by pioneering mass advertising techniques in Britain.
Lever soon began "vertical expansion," pushing into the British
retail trade to secure outlets for his products, and pushing into West
Africa to secure trading firms which could supply the palm oil. By
1922 he had bought out the Niger Company (which continued
as a trading company in northern Nigeria after the loss of its
charter), the African Association, Miller Brothers of Glasgow, and
several smaller firms, which were formed into the United Africa
Company as a subsidiary of the Lever interests. Only one substantial
British firm trading to West Africa, the Liverpool firm of John Holt
and Company, retained its independent position, though some
Syrian and Indian traders entered the field on a small scale.

If Africans were shut out from wholesaling and import-export trade by these large firms, they remained in control of the land and the system of production. Lever hoped to extend his vertical control down to the actual process of producing palm oil. He had powerful arguments in his favor, for the African system of collecting palm fruit was haphazard: there was practically no systematic breeding and cultivation of the palms, and the extraction of the oil was extremely wasteful. The Dutch had established European owned palm plantations in the East Indies, and Lever warned that if modern methods were not adopted, the Nigerian palm oil industry might be ruined. He demanded concessions of land for palm plantations, government assistance to provide a labor supply, and regulations fixing the price at which Africans should sell oil to crushing mills.

The British government supported its officials on the spot in resisting any such development. It was felt that the introduction of plantation production would create worse problems than it solved by producing a landless proletariat which would be divorced from traditional social life and organization, and which might become unemployed and destitute in time of slump. The British also felt that any attempt to alienate African land for plantation agriculture would provoke dangerous revolts and disaffection, and that it was simpler to leave palm oil production, however inefficient, in African hands. Lever finally abandoned the effort to secure concession in British West Africa, and secured them instead in the Belgian Congo.

The British attitude was in the long run justified, for palm oil production was for most Africans an additional cash income to subsistence farming. They were thus able to cushion the impact of lower market prices in time of glut, or even to stop producing altogether if prices fell too low, without widespread social dislocation or poverty emerging. In the event, African production of palm oil continued to expand, and Nigeria's exports of palm oil rose from £681,000 in 1900 to £1,634,000 in 1914. Palm kernels, increasingly used to produce oil used in margarine manufacture, rose from a value of £834,000 in 1900 to over £2.5 million in 1914.

The sale of palm products and the short-lived rubber boom in the Gold Coast at the end of the nineteenth century were merely extensions of the traditional African methods of securing imports by collecting produce. They did nothing to alter the basic pattern of subsistence farming. With the advent of colonial rule, settled administration, and the adoption of currency and more elaborate wants, some Africans now began to abandon, or partially abandon, the production of their own food in favor of cultivating cash crops for export. This was, indeed, a basic social change, for it extended the cash nexus, hitherto complete only among traders, or salaried and wage-earning Africans, into some of the rural areas. As the farmer turned to production for cash, he began to put monetary value on land, and to buy and sell it—a thing unknown in traditional life where land was held communally. He also began to employ labor and to pay wages himself. He became interested in taxes and customs duties, in the work of the government agricultural departments, and inevitably, in politics.

The British hoped that cotton would become such a cash crop grown by Africans, and efforts were made to promote its growth in Yorubaland adjacent to the railway line, with some success. The linking of Lagos and Kano by rail after 1911 gave the northern Nigerian peasant farmer the opportunity of marketing ground nuts, which developed to be worth £179,000 in 1914, and eventually became the north's chief export, accounting for a sixth of Nigeria's total export trade in the 1950s. But the most spectacular development of cash agriculture, the development of cocoa farming, was unforeseen by the British, and came as a result of a spontaneous African movement.

The Basel missionaries in the Gold Coast had tried to introduce cocoa cultivation in 1858, but had failed. In 1879 a Gold Coast laborer, Tetteh Quarshie, brought cocoa back to his home from Fernando Po. By 1895 Gold Coast farmers exported thirteen tons, and by 1905 exports had leaped to 5,000 tons; thereafter the figures doubled and redoubled until in 1911 the Gold Coast became the world's leading cocoa producer, exporting 40,000 tons of cocoa worth over £1.5 million. Cocoa now outstripped gold as the country's chief industry, and the values continued to rise. The fact that firms bearing the revered names of British Quaker families like Cadbury's, Rowntree's, and Fry's were building up a vast market for an African Negro farmers' product in Britain and Europe would have gladdened the hearts of the eighteenth-century Quaker abolitionists! The phenomenal growth continued after World War I, despite serious outbreaks of swollen shoot disease. By 1951 cocoa exports were worth

£60 million, and comprised more than 60 per cent of the country's export trade. Though cocoa growing developed in the Yoruba areas of Nigeria also, it never attained the scale of the industry in the Gold Coast. The Gold Coast cocoa industry had the effect of completely altering the relative positions of Nigeria and the Gold Coast. In 1900 Nigeria had been clearly regarded as a much more important area of prospective development, with its huge population and already established palm products trade; by 1910 Gold Coast development was clearly outstripping Nigeria's, showing the advantages of compact settlement and intensive railway development. By 1957, with only an eighth of Nigeria's population, Ghana's total exports were worth £86.5 million as compared with Nigeria's £132 million.

The Structure and Spirit of British Administration

The early British colonial regimes in the Gold Coast and Lagos began administration with few preconceived notions, except those arising from the policy of "legitimate commerce" which presupposed that the object of policy was to abolish slavery within the colony area, discourage slavery and the slave trade in neighboring African states, and develop commerce. It was natural that the educated elements among Africans should be regarded as allies in this task, and from 1860 to 1880 Africans rose to high positions in the colonial service. The British also brought with them institutions carried over from other colonial territories. The governor was expected to execute policy with the advice of his executive council, composed of the chief officials, and could legislate only with the approval of the legislative council. Though both of these councils were entirely nominated at first, it was a tradition of British colonial history that the legislative council was an embryonic parliament which in the course of time would become increasingly representative and eventually elected, and that when this stage was reached the executive council would gradually be transformed into a cabinet of ministers, responsible to the legislative council. Educated Africans were well aware of the history of the development of legislatures in Canada, Australia, and New Zealand, and never ceased to regard the legislative council as potentially the central and most important institution in the colony. By the 1890s the legislative councils of the Gold

Coast and Lagos both had educated African members, though these were nominated and not elected.

During the period of partition, however, the British began to change their attitude toward administrative policies, partly as a result of the growth during the 1870s and 1880s of ideas of Negro racial inferiority, expressed in pseudo-Darwinian terms. Such ideas among Europeans were intensified by the competitiveness of the educated Africans, whose ambition was to show themselves as capable of doing jobs normally done by Europeans. With improved medical conditions for Europeans after 1897, white officers began to bring out their wives and children, and to build a separate and exclusive social life of their own. Africans thus found promotion, especially to key posts, much more difficult.

The growing tension between the British and the educated Africans was not, however, purely a result of racialism. With the rapid occupation of the interior between 1880 and 1900, the British had to face the immediate problem of how to administer these areas. To build an elaborate network of direct administration through district officers would have been far too expensive, and the obvious solution was to maintain the traditional rulers as instruments of local government. The traditional authorities were on the whole hostile to educated Africans, and regarded them as low-born, upstart, and foreign. Moreover, the accession of so much territory at once made the educated elements, which were almost entirely coastal and urban, no longer representative of Africans in the new larger colonial areas. The British, therefore, called a halt to the development of the legislative councils. Though some educated Africans continued to be nominated to them, there was no move to introduce the elective principle. But much more serious from a "national" point of view was the fact that the competence of the legislative council's powers was not extended to all the newly acquired areas. The Niger Company never saw fit to summon a council, and when Lugard took over northern Nigeria it remained a separate protectorate outside the control of the Lagos legislative council, as did southern Nigeria (the former Niger Coast Protectorate) until 1906.

The British, in fact, had moved to a position in which they had decided to rest their authority on that of the traditional rulers, and to abandon educated Africans as "agents of civilization." There was thus a complete reversal of the situation before colonial times, in which it was traditional rulers like the Fulani, the Yoruba *obas*, or King Ja Ja who resisted British penetration, and the educated elements who undermined their resistance. The concept of indirect rule in West Africa developed especially in Nigeria, where it was to reach its classical form in the north. The Royal Niger Company had already advocated such a system of rule through the existing African authorities (though the Company's stand was as much an attempt to disguise its lack of effective authority as it was an administrative theory). Lugard, who had worked for the company in 1894, and had experience of similar systems in India and Uganda, developed the concept into an effective system of government. In his military campaigns against the Fulani rulers he was careful to emphasize that his object was to establish a British title to sovereignty and to depose uncooperative *emirs*, but he made no attempt to use the Hausa pretenders to the kingships existing before the *jihad*. When *emirs* were deposed they were replaced by more cooperative members of the same ruling family. Lugard made it clear that there would be no interference with Islam or Moslem law, that the existing Moslem courts would continue, as would the *emir's* administration. The Fulani rulers soon realized that the imposition of colonial rule was, in fact, to their advantage, for now that they were sanctioned in office by the British they could scarcely be overthrown by popular revolt.

The essential spirit of indirect rule was one of conservative reform. The traditional ruler was constituted as a "native authority," and each native authority was "advised" by a British officer (usually styled a resident in the emirates) who would only assert his powers in a critical or dangerous situation. Normally he would assert influence rather than give commands. At the same time, it was not intended that things should be frozen as they were for all time. The traditional authorities themselves would, in response to British advice, control the impact of modernity and thus avoid revolutionary tensions and upheavals. Much of this progress would come from the central colonial administration with its health and agricultural departments, railway administration, and other technical services, but the native authority had its own role too. Here the key institution was that of the native treasury, developed in northern Nigeria by Lugard. The complex Fulani taxes were replaced by a single tax levied on every village, but assessed by the British so as to prevent extortion. The native authority officials then collected the taxes, keeping detailed records and receipts which were audited by British officers. A fixed proportion of the receipts (the ideal was regarded as 50 per cent) was paid to the colonial government, while the rest could be spent locally on public projects determined by the *emir's* government. This was regarded by the British as an excellent training in self-government.

As a practical system of administration, indirect rule worked extremely well in northern Nigeria—so much so that the British began to believe that they had found the secret of ruling African peoples. Few British officers were aware that there were special reasons operative in the Fulani emirates which made the system a success, and which were not typical of normal African conditions. One of these was the important fact that the Fulani were recent conquerors anxious to stablize their position. Another was that the Fulani system of government was feudalistic, and it was thus easy for them to accept the idea of British overall suzerainty, which fitted in perfectly with their own political thinking. The British predilection for indirect rule was also a reflection of the growing disillusionment of many British officers with European society, for as the palmy days of Victorian self-confidence were passing away, industrial capitalism began to pass through series of slumps with huge levels of unemployment, and many began to feel that traditional African society possessed values and virtues which ought not to be destroyed. A kind of fanaticism for indirect rule was particularly noticeable after Lugard left northern Nigeria to become governor of Hong Kong in 1906.

The development of indirect rule in the north was undoubtedly a factor working to perpetuate the cultural gap between north and south. The northern government discouraged Christian missionaries, and the continued control of the Fulani rulers effectively prevented the development of a northern educated élite. Meanwhile, colonial rule in the south brought an intense flowering of missionary activity and a rapid growth of literate people. More and more excluded from the higher ranks of the administration (although thousands were employed as clerks by the government), the more ambitious Africans moved into the professions of journalism and the law, as well as teaching, the priesthood, and medicine. Their Mecca was Lagos, where the greatest economic opportunity existed, and they began to look to Lagos as the capital of Nigeria. They believed in the unification of the whole country, hoping that Lagos would emerge paramount from such a union, and extend the "progress" of the south into the "backward" north. For them the process seemed to be beginning when in 1906 the southeast and southwest were united as the Colony and Protectorate of Southern Nigeria, with Lagos as the seat of a single governor. The British government also wished for unification, for northern Nigerian administrative costs far exceeded revenue and had to be subsidized by the British taxpayer, whereas southern Nigeria accumulated surpluses. In 1912 Lugard was summoned back from Hong Kong, made governor-general of the whole of Nigeria, and given instructions to prepare a scheme of amalgamation.

When Lugard carried through his amalgamation in 1914 it became clear that, far from letting the south at last absorb the north, Lugard intended to use amalgamation to reinforce the forces of traditionalism throughout the country. The legislative council, which after 1906 had legislated for all southern Nigeria, was now restricted in competence to Lagos alone, and thus turned into little more than a municipal organ. There was obviously a clear intention that future evolution would not be along parliamentary lines. A Nigeria council was set up in its place, with three nominated Africans from the north and three from the south, but it was purely advisory with no legislative powers, and subsequently proved so unwieldy that it died a natural death. Only technical departments such as posts, railways, survey, military, treasury, and audit were made Nigeria-wide; in fact, separate governments for north and south Nigeria were kept in being under lieutenant-governors. The south gained nothing from amalgamation; there was no attempt to return Ilorin to its orbit, or still less to detach the non-Muslim areas from the north, and now the south had to contribute the bulk of northern administrative costs. Lugard even planned to abandon Lagos as the capital and establish the central government in the north, but was never able to accomplish this.

Worse was to follow for the southern educated elements, for Lugard was bent on introducing "native administration" into the south so as to bring local government into line with the northern system. The south was carved up into provinces, with "residents" stationed in each provincial capital. A new judicial organization was established, with "native courts" administering customary law with appeals to the provincial courts, and barristers were not allowed to plead in either, on the theory that English-trained lawyers would divert customary law along English lines. This naturally angered the Nigerian legal profession, especially as legal practice was now the most lucrative and prestigious profession open to Nigerians. Lugard then turned to introduce the actual system of native administration and indirect rule in the south. Richmond Palmer, a northern resident, toured the Yoruba states and reported that native treasuries and taxation ought to be begun. This was tantamount to arguing that Yoruba rulers could be made to correspond to northern *emirs*. The first attempt to establish the northern system was at Benin, whose *oba* had died in exile since its conquest in 1897. His son was restored, and direct taxation was begun at the same time, passing off without incident in the general goodwill of the restoration. In 1916 the system was extended to Oyo, where Lugard hoped to recreate the *alafin's* ancient supremacy as a paramount ruler. Here the first signs of serious opposition began to show themselves when four officials of the Oyo native authority were murdered at Iseyin in 1916.

The Yoruba rulers were naturally not averse to these attempts to restore their prerogatives, dignity, and wealth. But to the population-at-large the policy made no sense at all, for the powers which Lugard was now trying to pass on to the *obas* were powers which had never been possessed by them in traditional society, and the power of direct taxation was completely novel. The central government in Lagos would have had more success if it had tried to levy direct taxes in the name of Britain, for at least then the population would have known that it would be spent for developmental purposes and government. Matters came to a head in Abeokuta, where in 1914 Lugard had engineered the destruction of the semi-autonomous Egba United Government, controlled by the educated elements, and then established a native authority under the traditional ruler, the *alake*. Direct taxation was introduced, and in 1918 rebellion broke out when the Egba tore up the railway track, looted the station and rolling stock, and almost killed the *alake*. A large force of colonial troops had to suppress the rebellion, and hundreds of lives were lost in the fighting. A Commission of Inquiry which later investigated (and which included a Nigerian lawyer) laid the blame squarely on the new administrative policy.

When the system of native administration was extended to eastern Nigeria, the results were even worse, although serious revolts did not occur until the 1920s, when once again direct taxation provided the spark. In the Ibo and Ibibio areas chiefs were unknown to traditional society, so the British began creating them artificially by issuing warrants to men they regarded as locally influential. The "warrant chiefs," without any traditional authority, and thus with no moral basis for their rule, turned out with few exceptions to be unscrupulous, corrupt, and self-seeking, and their dishonesty and intimidation was exceeded only by the semi-educated clerks who kept the records of the so-called native courts. In 1929 the situation finally provoked widespread rioting in and around the town of Aba.

Despite these violent reactions, the British refused to accept the idea that there was any fundamental fault in the indirect rule system; they were firmly convinced that the theory was correct, and that faulty practice was responsible for any difficulties. The British re-action was to bring in anthropologists to investigate societies like the Ibo, and to advise where the true source of power lay. The work of the anthropologists, and the detailed adjustments to the system which resulted, undoubtedly did much to improve the situation, but few of the anthropologists had any concept of "primitive societies" being other than static, whereas these were in fact communities in motion which needed radical and novel institutions. At the national level Governor Sir Donald Cameron, who assumed office in 1930, also did much to remove anomalies. He attempted to produce more enlightenment in the northern emirates by encouraging *emirs* to travel in the south; he abolished the lieutenant-governor's office, and virtually abolished Lugard's judicial system in the south by restricting the powers of native courts, abolishing the provincial courts, and establishing appeals to a high court in which barristers could plead. Nevertheless, fundamentally British policy remained that of indirect rule until after World War II.

In the Gold Coast the British were equally concerned with preserving the status and dignity of the traditional authorities, but an indirect rule policy was virtually impossible, except in the Muslim states of the north, for a basic premise of the system was that the chief in the indirect rule system must be, in the last resort, under the control of the colonial regime. In the Akan states of the south this was scarcely possible, for the chief, in order to be accepted as "traditional," needed to be selected by the proper constitutional procedures, and the candidate thus selected might not necessarily be "sound" from the British viewpoint. Further contributing to the chaos was the fact that a chief who was satisfactory to the British was likely to prove unpopular with the people, and could, according to tradition, be easily "destooled." Destoolment in fact became increasingly common with the spread of indirect rule concepts in the Gold Coast, until the situation became almost farcical. Under such conditions the introduction of direct taxation was virtually impossible, and thus native treasuries, regarded as the keystone of the system, were never properly established.

Nevertheless, the British increasingly stressed their intention to preserve chieftaincy in the Gold Coast after 1910. "Native jurisdiction" questions provided a field for battles with the educated elements, and on several occasions the British had to amend, or even drop, proposed legislation attempting to revive or reorganize native courts. The attitude of the educated Gold Coastans, however, differed somewhat from that of the Nigerians, for their methods of selection and deposition of chiefs meant that they were much more open to pressures from the educated elements, and, indeed, several chiefs were themselves educated men, unlike the vast majority of Nigerian chiefs. The educated elements were thus not opposed to the honor and dignity of chiefs, but resisted any developments tending to make "native authorities" the sole mode of African political expression, or to downgrade the role of the legislative council or the colonial courts.

In 1924 the British inaugurated what was intended to develop into a new indirect rule policy in Ashanti. In the 1920s the anthropologist R. S. Rattray began publishing voluminous researches on Ashanti history and institutions, and reported that the deportation of Prempeh and the destruction of Ashanti chieftaincy was creating a dangerously anarchic situation. In 1924 minor powers of jurisdiction were restored to the Ashanti chiefs, and Prempeh was allowed to return from exile as a private citizen. In 1926 Prempeh was recognized as *kumasihene*, i.e., chief of Kumasi alone, and after his death his successor was restored as *asantehene* in 1935. At the same time the old Ashanti council was revived as the Ashanti Confederacy Council and treated by the British as a kind of "national" parliament of Ashanti. These moves were paralleled by less dramatic developments in the states to the south with the steady creation after 1925 of provincial councils of chiefs. From this time the British openly declared their policy to be basically one of indirect rule, and the educated elements began to rally in opposition to the political influence of chiefs.

The Development of African Nationalism

African nationalism is sometimes explained as simply an inevitable movement of opposition to "colonialism," but such an explanation skirts the essential nature of the movement. In the period of partition from 1880 to 1900 it was the traditional rulers who put up the strongest opposition to the assertion of colonial rule, while at no time in the history of nationalism in the Gold Coast or Nigeria were the nationalist groups willing to organize violent revolution. In fact, before the 1930s they were not even opposed to the fundamental nature of colonial rule, but only to certain aspects of colonial practice. The essence of African nationalism lay not in its negative anti-colonialism but in its positive set of attitudes concerning the nature of the African, his relationship to the family of mankind, and his proper social and political organization. The political theory through which these ideas were expressed was a complex blend of influences, the majority of which came from Europe and America. The French and American revolutionary traditions, the humanitarian anti-slavery doctrines, and the principles of English common law all made their contributions, and later the doctrines of socialism were grafted on. The aim of the nationalists was the creation of new African Negro nations, controlled by a democratic citizenry of equals, which would enter the family of nations as independent states which could demonstrate to the world the capacities of the Negro race.

The humanitarian doctrines of "Commerce and Christianity"

admirably fitted these goals, and the first generation of English-
educated Africans like Crowther felt that the British were their
allies in the regeneration of Africa. The first rift came with the
growth of ideas of racial inferiority in Europe, and in the 1860s and
1870s men like Edward Wilmot Blyden (a West Indian who had
adopted Liberia as his home) and the Gold Coast doctor J. Africanus
Horton developed the earliest nationalist literature in their efforts
to assert the innate rationality of the West African Negro by inter-
preting his history, customs, and institutions. In this period men
visualized that the goal of creating new nations could be achieved
over a long period of time by the gradual reform of existing African
states (as in the Mankessim movement in the Gold Coast) and
through African organized missions like the CMS Niger Mission under
Bishop Crowther. But when the British swung over to the rapid
extension of their colonial territory after 1880 the general reaction
was one of joy rather than alarm, for the nationalists could envisage
the British creating in decades the structure of large "national"
units, cutting rapidly through the resistance of African sovereign
units which might have taken centuries to federate and reform. The
inheritance, they were sure, would be theirs, for the history of the
British Empire (which rapidly became a standard part of school
history syllabuses in West Africa) showed that British colonies
inevitably evolved into self-governing dominions.

Nevertheless, there was plenty of scope for criticism of British
actions, as the exclusion of Africans from higher administrative posts
and the consequent drift of the ablest into journalism and the law
(both professions which feed on grievance) led to an assertive development of African political views. In the Gold Coast a British
attempt to gain control of land sales in an effort to control anarchic
alienation of land to gold mining companies, led to the creation of
the Aborigines' Rights Protection Society in 1897, which remained
in being as a focus for agitation (much of it successful) on many
detailed issues of Gold Coast administration for many years.

Nationalism also began to assert itself in the religious sphere.
Crowther's elevation to the bishopric in 1864 had been opposed from
the first by some of the white clergy, and from 1880 they began
mounting attacks upon his Niger Mission. Scandals among African
clergy on the Niger helped to undermine Crowther's authority. In

1890 local white missionaries succeeded in carrying through a purge of the mission, and when Bishop Crowther died in 1891, in the midst of the crisis which this caused, the African clergy broke away to form the United African Native Church. In 1888 a similar break-away African Baptist Church had also been formed for similar reasons. Though the United African Native Church was later reconciled with the Church of England, the revolt began a movement of independence in religious matters which thereafter resulted in the foundation of several new religious groups. All of them stressed "independent government" as their aim, many went further by asserting that Africans must adapt Christianity to local conditions, and for the extremists Christ became a black man, and polygamy was allowed.

In political affairs, however, there was little of this extremism. Movements like the Aborigines' Rights Protection Society were essentially intellectual, had practically no mass organization, and functioned more as social clubs and debating societies than as political parties. The First World War carried political organization onto a new plain, and stimulated nationalist hopes. The allied war propaganda had stressed the "fight for democracy" and the rights of small nations, and during the war the British had promised eventual self-government for India. Gold Coast and Nigerian troops fought against the Germans in Togo, the Cameroons, and East Africa, and the conquered German colonies were divided after the war between Britain and France, with parts of the Cameroons being attached to Nigeria and Togo to the Gold Coast as "mandates" held in trust for the benefit of their populations under the League of Nations. The intellectual leaders in all the British West African colonies came together in 1920 to form the National Congress of British West Africa. The program of the congress supplies an interesting barometer of the state of political nationalism. As yet there was no Gold Coast or Nigerian nationalism as such; the leaders looked to the whole of British West Africa as their unit, and attempted to secure not self-government, but policies which would divert attention from the indirect rule policy and place effective control in the hands of the legislative councils. They thus demanded a clear assertion that future development would be toward the goal of a self-governing dominion of British West Africa. They asked that half the members of each legislative council be elected Africans, that the councils control taxation, that chiefs be appointed and dismissed by their own people as in the Akan states, that racial discrimination in the civil service end, and that a university be founded.

The British authorities treated the congress with scant respect, and refused to be deflected from the development of indirect rule. Governor Clifford of Nigeria dismissed the members of the congress as unrepresentative of Africans; their British education, he asserted, made them virtually foreigners, and their idea of a West African nation he dismissed as "an absurdity," at least "in the visible future." Despite this apparent contempt for their views, the British did concede, although on a very limited scale, the vitally important principle of elections. In Nigeria in 1922 the legislative council was recast so that two members from Lagos and one from Calabar were to be elected by adult males with £100 a year income. The concession led to the formation of the Nigerian National Democratic Party, led by Herbert Macaulay (a relative of Bishop Crowther), which won all the elected seats until after 1933. In the Gold Coast the legislative council was recast in 1925 and similarly elected members from Sekondi, Accra, and Cape Coast were admitted.

Until World War II this was the most the British were prepared to concede, faced as they were with acute economic difficulties during the great depression. The British-educated African leadership was unable and unwilling to make any serious challenge, though they continued to grumble, debate, and publish. In the late 1930s the masses, especially the semi-literate cocoa farmers and wage earners, began to stir in response to economic difficulties, attempting to force up prices by combination among growers, to reduce import prices by boycott, and to form trade unions to improve wages. The intellectual nationalists were unwilling to assume leadership of these developments. Many of them felt that the masses were far from ready for political power, and in any case the appeal of the British-trained élite, who were fond of parading their subtle erudition and scholarship, was hardly what the masses required.

A new leadership, nevertheless, came forward and was provided largely by American-trained graduates. Entry to British universities had always been difficult—there were few enough places even for British students—and students were not allowed to secure paid employment during university terms, so that study in Britain was expensive. In the 1920s students from Nigeria and the Gold Coast began entering the American Negro universities, where they were often much better qualified than American students, and where they could work their way through college. American education produced a different type of graduate, whose standard of education was much lower than that of the British-trained, but who did not have imparted to him an automatic sense of belonging to a privileged élite. On return to the Gold Coast or Nigeria, the American-trained graduate often found himself dismissed by his British-trained counterpart as "semi-literate" and the recipient of a "cheap degree."

But the American-educated Africans had a different attitude to the masses, and were impatient with the cautious approach of the old élite. If their education was crude and lacking in subtlety, this of itself allowed them to communicate with a mass African audience in a new style. They thus turned to the creation of a new journalism —no longer aimed at respectable salaried "collar and tie" Africans— which was racy, irreverent, often ungrammatical, but which would be read by the mass products of the mission schools who had no higher education.

It is no coincidence, therefore, that the presidents of both Nigeria and Ghana are graduates of American universities. Nnamdi Azikiwe was the pioneer of this development. In 1935 Azikiwe returned from the United States and settled in the Gold Coast, where there was a greater literacy rate than his native Nigeria, to begin his journalistic career. In 1937 he went back to Nigeria and founded the *West African Pilot*, which was to become the leading Nigerian organ of nationalist opinion for twenty years. Azikiwe also supported the Nigerian Youth Movement, founded in 1936, which he helped to transform from a local Lagos affair into a widespread southern organization incorporating Yorubas and Ibos. "Zik" and his triumphant return inspired Kwame Nkrumah, then a young teacher in training, to leave for America in 1937 where he studied first at Lincoln and then at the University of Pennsylvania, working his way through both institutions and becoming president of the African Students' Organization of North America.

World War II intensified the nationalist ferment to an unprecedented height and gave the movement a much wider basis. Large numbers of Gold Coast and Nigerian troops saw action in the Far East against the Japanese, and for the first time Africans assumed commands as commissioned officers. At the same time British soldiers and airmen came to both countries, and many Africans were made to realize for the first time that there were unprivileged Englishmen who were factory workers, shopkeepers, and private soldiers. These British troops, who were mostly conscripts, remained outside the "colonial" European community and mixed freely with Africans in the towns, some of them even taking part in left wing trade unionism and political activity. The war itself was pictured in allied propaganda as a war against German racialism and Japanese imperialism, and the Atlantic Charter asserted the right of all peoples to choose their own form of government. In Britain Churchill's coalition government included the Labor Party whose members pressed for a clear declaration that postwar colonial policies in West Africa would be directed toward planned social and economic progress and political advance to self-government. In 1944 Azikiwe took the lead in forming the National Council of Nigeria and the Cameroons (NCNC), intended to become a mass party. The conservative intellectuals in the Gold Coast, led by J. B. Danquah, now tried to bid for mass support with their United Gold Coast Convention (UGCC), and in 1947 they called home Kwame Nkrumah to become its organizing secretary.

During 1948 the Gold Coast was swept by unrest which boiled over into violence. There was a well organized boycott of European traders, and the ex-servicemen returned home to demand some reward for fighting the Empire's wars. Demonstrations by ex-servicemen led to rioting in Accra and other major cities which was put down with loss of life. The Watson Commission which inquired into the situation reported that only political advance of a spectacular kind would stabilize the situation. The British Labor government was prepared to do so, and took the unprecedented step of appointing an all-African committee (known as the Coussey Committee) to work out a new constitution. The committee was naturally composed of the more experienced and elderly African leaders, and worked for a transitional constitution to give Africans experience of self-government while leaving reserve powers to the British. The UGCC and Danquah supported this concept. This was the signal for Nkrumah to break with the UGCC, and he split away and formed the Convention People's Party (CPP) with the slogan "self-government *now*." This was a far more effective appeal than that of the UGCC, and Nkrumah's position was further assisted when he and other CPP leaders were arrested for their "positive action" policies of fomenting strikes and riots. Those who had served their time proudly wore their prison caps after release and added the "degree" of P.G. (prison graduate) after their names.

Nkrumah was still in prison when the elections were held in 1951 under the new constitution which was the result of the Coussey Committee's report. The constitution fell far short of self-government, but the elected members were made predominant in the legislature, and members of the majority party would for the first time take ministerial office in the executive council. The CPP defeated the UGCC with ease in the directly elected seats, and Arden-Clarke, the new governor, released Nkrumah from prison and brought him and other CPP leaders into ministerial office. Nkrumah and the CPP began almost immediately to press the British for further advance, and the British finally agreed to accept full responsible government after elections demonstrating the wish of the mass of the people for it. These were held in June 1954, when the CPP won 71 of the assembly's 104 seats, all of which were now directly elective.

Self-government was further delayed, however, by the sudden emergence of a powerful opposition movement based on Ashanti. Popular support for the new opposition came from the disgruntled cocoa farmers, who were incensed at the low price fixed by the government's cocoa marketing board. This disaffection was welded together by Dr. K. A. Busia, a prominent Ashanti intellectual, and openly supported by the *asantehene*. It was significantly named the National Liberation Movement, and demanded a federal form of government before British withdrawal. Against bitter protests from Nkrumah, the British insisted on the holding of a third election, which followed the United Nations plebiscite in the Gold Coast administered area of Togo which had voted for integration in June 1956. In July the final election of the colonial period gave Nkrumah and the CPP 72 of the 104 seats, much the same overall result as in 1954. Regionally, however, the picture was worse for the CPP, for it won only eight of the twenty-one Ashanti seats, and only eleven of the twenty-six northern seats. A case could thus be made either that the nation as a whole rejected federalism, or that the regions from which the demand for federalism had come clearly wanted it. The British now succeeded in affecting the curious compromise whereby the regional assemblies were set up, without any division of sovereignty with the central government, and on March 6, 1957, the Gold Coast became independent with the new name of Ghana.

The postwar political development in Nigeria seemed to begin in much the same way as that of the Gold Coast, with Azikiwe's NCNC forcing the pace, and the British attempting to ensure a smooth transition by pouring millions of pounds into economic development while limiting the development of the legislative council. In 1947 a new constitution at last extended the competence of the legislative council to include northern Nigeria and established a majority of Nigerian representatives, but only four members were directly elected. Sir John Macpherson, who became governor in 1948, immediately embarked on further advance, and called a series of national and regional conferences of Nigerians in 1949 to shape the new system. These discussions perhaps for the first time made Nigerian leaders face up to the very difficult problems of harmonizing the widely differing linguistic, cultural, and religious differences in the country, and this in turn brought "tribalism" (already in evidence after 1945 in the formation of tribal unions such as the Ibo State Union and the Egbe Omo Oduduwa among the Yorubas) onto the political scene. The northern emirs, sensing the shape of things to come, formed the Northern Peoples' Congress (NPC), while the rivalry of Ibo and Yoruba increasingly turned the NCNC into an Ibo instrument, and led to the formation of the Action Group (AG) as a Yoruba party under Chief Awolowo. None of these groups came out firmly, as the CPP had done in the Gold Coast, for a unitary state, for this was clearly impossible. The differences were essentially of emphasis, the NCNC wanting a large number of regions so as to produce a strong central government, the AG and NPC wanting to preserve the Yoruba and Hausa-Fulani areas as single units, and thus arguing for large regions, few in number. A new constitution finally emerged in 1951, establishing regional legislatures in east, west, and north Nigeria. It fell far short of self-government, for the central legislature was composed largely of indirectly elected representatives, but it at least gave experience of ministerial office to Nigerians at the federal and regional levels.

As long as the 1951 constitution operated the southern parties found a basis for cooperation against its limited scope. In 1954, after conferences in Nigeria and London of the main political leaders, the British finally agreed to establish a full federal system, with the central legislature fully elected and controlling the appointment of some of the federal ministers, and with similar arrangements for the regional assemblies. From 1954 to 1960 the struggle for full self-government and independence became a struggle among the Nigerian politicians rather than against the British, and one in which one of the chief elements of delay was the lack of mass political organization and administrative experience in the north. In 1957, as the result of a further conference in London with the Nigerian political leaders, the office of federal prime minister was created, and the eastern and western regions became fully self-governing in internal affairs. The northern region followed suit in 1959, after the resumed constitutional conference had agreed in 1958 on the broad basis of a final federal constitution for an independent Nigeria. In 1959 federal elections were held in which the NPC won 149 seats (142 of them in the north), and the NCNC and its allies won eighty-nine (fifty-eight of these in the east, twenty-three in the west, and eight in the north) and the Action Group won seventy-five (thirty-six in the west, twenty-four in the north, and fifteen in the east). The temptation for the southern parties to form a coalition and force the northerners into opposition was avoided, and the NCNC and NPC allied to form the government, with Alhaji Tafawa Balewa as prime minister. Dr. Azikiwe became president of the senate, and was nominated governor-general by the British upon independence in 1960.

The African political scene moves so rapidly that it is difficult to suggest literature on the current scene which will not be rapidly dated. However, Rupert Emerson & Martin Kilson, *The Political Awakening of Africa*, Ken Post's *The New States of West Africa** (Harmondsworth, 1964), Dennis Austin's *Politics in Ghana, 1946-1960* (London, 1964), R. O. Tilman and T. Cole's *The Nigerian Political Scene* (Durham, N.C., 1962) and James Coleman's *Nigeria, Background to Nationalism* (Berkeley and Los Angeles, 1958) are all works of permanent value.

Anyone who wishes to place the history of these countries within the overall perspective of African history could not do better than to digest Roland Oliver and J. D. Fage, *A Short History of Africa** (Harmondsworth, 1962) which can be used in conjunction with J. D. Fage, *An Atlas of African History* (London, 1958). The same author's *An Introduction to the History of West Africa* (third edition, Cambridge, 1962) deals with West Africa in more detail. Still the best general history of Ghana is W. E. F. Ward's *A History of Ghana* (revised second edition, London, 1958), while Freda Wolfson, *Pagent of Ghana* (London, 1958) has provided a useful set of extracts from contemporary sources. M. Crowder's *The Story of Nigeria* (London, 1957) is easily the best general history of Nigeria, and it is admirably supplemented by the collection of documents, *Nigerian Perspectives* (London, 1960) by Thomas Hodgkin, which contains a brilliant introductory essay. Those who wish to penetrate deeper into historical study and to keep up with current research in progress should follow the *Journal of the Historical Society of Nigeria* and the *Transactions of the Historical Society of Ghana*. Important articles on Nigerian and Ghanaian history also appear in the *Journal of African History*.

For the early history of development prior to contact with Europe,

* Books marked with an asterisk are in paperback editions.

G. P. Murdoch's *Africa, Its People and Their Culture History* (New York, 1959) should be treated with caution, but is a stimulating interpretation, and its index allows the reader to find rapidly a description of almost any African linguistic group. For the significance of language in relation to history the serious student must consult J. H. Greenberg, *Studies in African Linguistic Classification* (New Haven, 1955). The best discussions of all these questions have occurred in the pages of the *Journal of African History*.

E. W. Bovill's *The Golden Trade of the Moors* (London, 1958) is a useful study of the links between North Africa and the savannah area down to the nineteenth century. Bornu is dealt with in detail by Y. Urvoy's *Histoire de l'empire de Bornou* (Paris, 1949). The nineteenth-century Nigerian scholar, the Reverend Samuel Johnson's *History of the Yorubas* (reprinted London, 1956) remains a classic attempt to distill oral traditions into history, as does the venerable Jacob Egharevba's *History of Benin* (third edition, Cambridge, 1960), which can be supplemented by R. E. Bradbury and P. C. Lloyd, *The Benin Kingdom* (London, 1959). I. Wilks, *The Northern Factor in Ashanti History* (Legon, 1961) throws completely new light on the origins and development of Ashanti.

Several of the above works discuss the effects of the slave trade on the internal development of African states. Still the best survey of the slave trade as a whole is the unfortunately rare work, H. A. Wyndham, *The Atlantic and Slavery* (London, 1935). J. W. Blake, *Europeans in West Africa, 1450-1560* (London, 1942) is a more detailed treatment of the earlier period of contact before slaving dominated normal trade. The pamphlet *Bahia and the West African Trade* by P. Verger (Ibadan, 1964) is a most useful study of the Brazilian role.

The nineteenth century and the transition to colonial rule has received much attention from scholars. Roland and Caroline Oliver's *Africa in the Days of Exploration* is a very useful anthology of travelers' accounts of pre-colonial Africa. K. O. Dike's *Trade and Politics in the Niger Delta, 1830-1885* (Oxford, 1957) is a brilliant study of the repercussions of the development of the palm oil trade. Another Nigerian scholar, S. O. Biobaku, deals with the missionary impact on Abeokuta in *The Egba and Their Neighbours, 1842-1872* (Oxford, 1957). C. W. Newbury's *The Western Slave Coast and Its Rulers* (Oxford, 1961) is a study of the coast between Ghana and Lagos. J. F. Ade Ajayi and R. S. Smith cooperated to produce the most interesting study, *Yoruba Warfare in the Nineteenth Century* (Cambridge and Ibadan, 1964). Philip Curtin's *The Image of Africa* (London, 1965) traces the development of British attitudes to the West African peoples from 1780 to 1850. The partition is analyzed in J. D. Hargreaves, *Prelude to the Partition in West Africa* (London, 1963). D. Kimble's *A Political History of Ghana 1850-1928* (Oxford, 1963) is a monumental and encyclopedic attempt to trace the complex interaction of British, Fante, and Ashanti in this period. J. E. Flint, *Sir George Goldie and the Making of Nigeria* (London, 1960) is a study of British policies in the partition period and of the history of the Royal Niger Company.

For the period of British colonial rule the classic work is Margery Perham's two volume biography *Lugard* (London, 1956 and 1960) and her study of *Native Administration in Nigeria* (reprinted Oxford, 1962) still has great value. Coleman's *Nigeria, Background to Nationalism*, already mentioned, is the most detailed treatment of the period since 1918. J. B. Webster's *The African Churches Among the Yoruba, 1888-1922* (Oxford, 1964) and J. F. A. Ajayi's *Christian Missions and Nigeria: The Making of a New Elite* (London, 1965) both illustrate in detail the theme of religious "nationalism." D. Apter, *The Gold Coast in Transition* (Princeton, 1955) is a sociological study of the twentieth century, with much brilliant analysis, but marred by desperate technical jargon. F. M. Bourret, *Ghana, the Road to Independence, 1919-1957* (London, 1960) is much simpler to read, but less stimulating. Polly Hill, *The Gold Coast Cocoa Farmer* (London, 1956) examines the effects of the cash economy on an important social group.

Sometimes the novel can provide insights impossible to obtain elsewhere. Joyce Cary spent much of his life as a British district officer before he became a novelist, and his *Mister Johnson** (London, 1939; paperback 1962) is a masterly characterization of the moral confusion produced by inadequate education on an African clerk. The finest Nigerian novelist is undoubtedly Chinua Achebe, who has set himself the task of portraying the themes of Nigerian history through the novel. His study of the disintegration of Ibo customary life in face of the missionary impact in *Things Fall Apart** (London, 1958; paperback 1962) is perhaps the finest novel by any African writer. Equally enthralling is his study of corruption and nepotism on the contemporary scene, *No Longer at Ease** (London, 1960; paperback 1963).

* Books marked with an asterisk are in paperback editions.

INDEX

169

British Authors in the Twentieth Century Views Series

American Authors in the Twentieth Century Views Series

European Authors in the Twentieth Century Views Series

The American Assembly Series

The Eyewitness Accounts of American History Series

The Modern Nations in Historical Perspective Series